Day by Day with God

January–April 2002

DAY BY DAY WITH GOD

Bible Readings for Women

JANUARY–APRIL 2002

Christina Press
BRF
Tunbridge Wells/Oxford

Bible Reading Fellowship
First Floor, Elsfield Hall, 15–17 Elsfield Way, Oxford OX2 8FG

First published in Great Britain 2002

ISBN 1 84101 164 9

Jacket design: JAC Design for Print, Crowborough

Trade representation in UK:
Lion Publishing plc, Peter's Way, Sandy Lane West,
Oxford OX4 6HG

Distributed in Australia by:
Willow Connection, PO Box 288, Brookvale, NSW 2100.
Tel: 02 9948 3957; Fax: 02 9948 8153;
E-mail: info@willowconnection.com.au

Distributed in New Zealand by:
Scripture Union Wholesale, PO Box 760, Wellington
Tel: 04 385 0421; Fax: 04 384 3990; E-mail: suwholesale@clear.net.nz

Distributed in South Africa by:
Struik Book Distributors, PO Box 193, Maitland 7405
Tel: 021 551 5900; Fax: 021 551 1124; E-mail: enquiries@struik.co.za

Acknowledgments
Scriptures from The New Revised Standard Version of the Bible,
Anglicized Edition, copyright © 1989, 1995 by the Division of
Christian Education of the National Council of the Churches of
Christ in the USA, used by permission. All rights reserved.

Scriptures from The Revised Standard Version of the Bible, copyright
© 1946, 1952, 1971 by the Division of Christian Education of the
National Council of the Churches of Christ in the USA, used by
permission. All rights reserved.

The Living Bible copyright © 1971 by Tyndale House Publishers.

Scripture quotations taken from The Holy Bible, New International
Version, copyright © 1973, 1978, 1984 by International Bible Society.
Used by permission of Hodder & Stoughton Ltd. All rights reserved.
'NIV' is a registered trademark of International Bible Society. UK
trademark number 1448790.

Extracts from the Authorized Version of the Bible (The King James
Bible), the rights in which are vested in the Crown, are reproduced by
permission of the Crown's Patentee, Cambridge University Press.

The Message © 1993 by Eugene H. Peterson, NavPress, Colorado
Springs

Printed in Great Britain by Bookmarque, Croydon

Contents

6 The Editor writes…

8 Contributors

10 A Morning Prayer

11 Moses   1–12 January
    Diana Archer

23 The community of the Church   13–26 January
    Beryl Adamsbaum

37 Acts 18—21   27 January–9 February
    Christina Rees

51 Who is in control?   10–23 February
    Chris Leonard

65 Food and faith   24 February–9 March
    Rosemary Green

79 Mother hen ministry   10–16 March
    Jennifer Rees Larcombe

86 Jesus and Lazarus   17–23 March
    Kristina Petersen

93 The Easter message   24 March–6 April
    Alie Stibbe

107 Confidence in God   7–13 April
    Christine Platt

114 1 Corinthians 7   14–20 April
    Anne Coomes

121 God and music   21–30 April
    Sandra Wheatley

131 Magazine section

156 Order forms

158 Subscription information

The Editor writes...

I remember being taught that when writing an article the first sentence was crucial. You had to grip the attention of your reader (or your publisher) immediately, then everything would just follow on. Well, I have been sitting here in front of my computer for ages trying first one introductory sentence for this letter, and then another, each attempt getting even more mundane than the one before! It is the beginning of a new year and I should be writing some wise words to begin this issue of *Day by Day with God*.

However, each of the notes on the following pages begin in exactly the right way—with a sentence from the Bible. What better way to start anything? And exactly the right way to start each day and help us to get God's perspective on whatever it holds for each one of us.

Points to ponder

Diana Archer has written the first notes for this new year, based on episodes from the life of Moses. Moses seems light years away from the year 2002—and yet from each story there is a valuable point to ponder that is relevant to life today. Have you ever noticed how many of the Gospel incidents recorded involve food? Rosemary Green's notes will provide spiritual sustenance as she focuses on Jesus either sharing meals with friends and followers, or using food as a teaching point. Then, in the Magazine section, Alie Stibbe has written an article that is intended to give us 'food for thought'. She voices her concern at the diet today's children are given through the media, music, books and so on—another form of food. This should not only give us food for thought but stir us into action where necessary!

Mothering Sunday

Jennifer Rees Larcombe begins her notes on Mothering Sunday, and she points out that this particular Sunday can be painful for some people. I certainly felt left out the first Mothering Sunday I went to without any children to bring me a posy of flowers! However, we have all had a mother, or mother figure, in our lives to remember on this special day—and there are many people around of all ages who need a bit of mothering when life gets tough! Margaret Killingray, in her article on the meaning of mothering, points out that in God's treatment of us we have a perfect example of true mothering, or parenting.

Thanks

My thanks to all who have written in with thoughts, comments and ideas. I had a letter this week from someone saying how much she had appreciated one particular set of notes and asking me to pass on her thanks to the writer. She added that she would go back to these notes again in a few months' time. It is always good to know that a writer's insights into a particular passage of the Bible have really been helpful to those who use *Day by Day with God*. I wonder how many more readers go back to particular notes they have found helpful. I have also heard that notes have been quoted in sermons and used in ladies' meetings and Bible studies.

I trust that you will enjoy using this issue of *Day by Day with God* as much as I have enjoyed editing it, and that each day you will find something to help you relate God's word to everyday life.

Mary Reid

Contributors

Beryl Adamsbaum is a language teacher living in France, just across the border from Geneva, Switzerland, where she and her husband have been engaged in Christian ministry for thirty years. She is involved in teaching, preaching and counselling. She is the editor of her church magazine and writes short devotional articles.

Diana Archer has three young children and a degree in religious studies. She has served as a missionary in Japan, worked as a freelance editor and writer, and written the highly acclaimed book *Who'd Plant a Church?* She now works with the Damaris Trust, producing home group Bible studies on the Internet.*

Anne Coomes has been a journalist for the Church of England for nearly twenty years. Together with the well-known artist Taffy Davies, she has launched www.parishpump.co.uk, a website providing articles for parish magazine editors. Anne also does freelance communications work for various dioceses, and has written five books. She holds a degree in theology and is Reader for her parish in north Cheshire.

Rosemary Green has an international speaking ministry, sometimes alongside her husband Michael. Her highly praised book *God's Catalyst* distils her wisdom and experience gained through many years of prayer counselling. She is on the pastoral staff of Wycliffe Theological College in Oxford.

Jennifer Rees Larcombe, one of Britain's best-loved Christian authors and speakers, lives in Kent. She contributes regularly to Christian magazines, including a problem page, and has recently published a book on the ministry of angels, a children's Bible story book and an account of her dramatic recovery, *Unexpected Healing*. Her latest book for BRF is *Beauty from Ashes*.

* Visit www.connectbiblestudies.com

Chris Leonard, her husband and two student-age children live in an untidy house in Surrey. Chris has a degree in English and theology and her twelve books range from biography and devotional to children's stories. She enjoys leading creative writing workshops because 'people are so interesting—and they grow!' Recent BRF publications include *The Heart of Christmas* and *The Road to Easter* (co-written with Jacqui Gardner).

Kristina Petersen is a member of staff at BRF. She lives in Oxford and is single. She has worked at Lee Abbey, the Christian holiday and conference centre in Devon, where she edited and wrote for their quarterly magazine *Rapport*.

Christine Platt worked for ten years with The Navigators, living in Ivory Coast and travelling widely throughout Africa. She is now a health visitor in Cardiff and writes booklets and articles. She has written the SU *Lifebuilder* Bible study book on 'Forgiveness'.

Christina Rees is a freelance writer and broadcaster, speaker, preacher and a member of the General Synod of the Church of England and the Archbishops' Council. She is also Chair of WATCH (Women and the Church), a national organization that provides a forum for promoting women in the Church. Her latest book is *The Divine Embrace*, about discovering the relevance of God's love.

Alie Stibbe has a degree in Natural Sciences and spent five years in medical research before beginning to write for *Renewal* and other Christian magazines. Alie is studying part-time towards an MA in Advanced Scandinavian Translation in London and teaches Norwegian for beginners at a local language centre. She is married to an Anglican minister and they have four children.

Sandra Wheatley lives in County Durham, is a qualified nurse and was diagnosed with multiple sclerosis fourteen years ago. She is single, lives alone, but is not lonely as family and friends live nearby. She has a variety of interests which keep her actively involved in the lives of those around her.

**Contributors are identified by their initials
at the bottom of each page.**

A Morning Prayer

Thank you, heavenly Father,
for this new day.
Be with me now
in all I do
and think
and say,
that it will be to your glory.

Amen

Start with Moses

The king of Egypt said to the Hebrew midwives, whose names were Shiphrah and Puah, 'When you help the Hebrew women in childbirth and observe them on the delivery stool, if it is a boy, kill him; but if it is a girl, let her live.' The midwives, however, feared God and did not do what the king of Egypt had told them to do; they let the boys live.

A new day, a new year, a new start. For those of us adept at muddling through life, we hope that perhaps this year we will be more ordered. Perhaps our walk with God will be more like a Roman road heading for heaven and less like a meandering country lane where we lose our perspective at every turn. So, where to start? Sorting the socks or two hours in prayer? Is that the telephone ringing? Oh, what does it matter anyway?

For all those unrealistic, easily-distracted dreamers out there like me, look at Shiphrah and Puah. We meet these two women at the start of the story of Moses, even before he was born. They were squashed between two male-dominated societies, with one, Egypt, enslaving the other, Israel. These midwives had no status, but the Bible singles them out because their actions were vital. Despite their vulnerability, they chose civil disobedience. By saving the boys' lives, they had a profound impact on the whole Hebrew nation, preventing its emasculation. What would have happened otherwise?

How did they change the course of history? By fearing God and doing their job well. Because God was the defining priority in their lives, they chose to obey him rather than Pharaoh. They continued to perform their job with integrity and to respect the sanctity of life. Thus they saved a nation.

Whatever your situation this New Year, be encouraged. You matter to God and your choices count. They may not have nation-saving status, but God can use everything.

Dear Father, teach me how to fear you, and help me to do my job well. Amen.

Read Lamentations 3:22–26.

DA

Superwomen

'Why have you done this? Why have you let the boys live?' The
midwives answered Pharaoh, 'Hebrew women are not like
Egyptian women; they are vigorous and give birth before the
midwives arrive.' So God was kind to the midwives and the
people increased and became even more numerous. And because
the midwives feared God, he gave them families of their own.

Day Two. New Year. I hope the novelty hasn't worn off yet. Seize the day!

As we dive into the early years of Moses' life, these preparatory events set the scene. Guess what—they all revolve around women! It is women who are the key players in this unfolding drama. Without these wonderful midwives, where would the Hebrew men have been? Now Shiphrah and Puah are face to face with Pharaoh. Was this a downright lie—that they never got to the action in time? Did the Hebrew women give birth faster than the Egyptians, so that this was just stretching the truth a little? Certainly the midwives must have been in league with the mothers, together determined to protect the innocent baby boys. For those of us who have borne children, the thought of doing so in such difficult circumstances is awesome. Was it really a case of, 'Push, push—before the midwives get here!'?

Whatever went on, it was the women who saved the day. They took incredible risks to protect human life. Their actions reflect those of all who, down the centuries, have tried to sabotage genocide. The biblical account here reiterates what motivated Shiphrah and Puah—the fear of the Lord.

'Fearing God' is not a phrase I hear very often. No one lately has asked me if I fear God. What does it mean, if it led these women into potential danger? It also led them to care for others. Where does the fear of the Lord lead you and me? Is God really number one in our lives, so that we will willingly follow that leading?

Lord, help me to be whole-hearted in following you. Amen.
DA

Moses afloat

She got a papyrus basket for [Moses] and coated it with tar and pitch. Then she placed the child in it and put it among the reeds along the bank of the Nile. His sister stood at a distance to see what would happen to him.

New Year day three. How many resolutions have flown out the window? Isn't it wonderful that God deals in grace?

Anyone who has been to a Sunday school worth its salt will be very familiar with the story of Moses. You have probably made/drawn/painted this very scene—a cute three-month-old gurgling in a miniature boat. Revisiting the plot with a more 'grown up' perspective adds depth to the drama.

It is the women again. Desperate to thwart Pharaoh's evil edict that all baby boys must now be thrown into the Nile, Moses' mother plans a possible escape. Moses' basket is placed near the princess's bathing haunt—surely this was strategic? Moses' sister is set on watch. How many nights had Moses' mother lain awake worrying before hitting on this idea? Her ingenuity had kept Moses alive so far. Would this new risk prove worth taking? In order to stand any chance of saving him, she had to give up her son.

All of us face impossible situations at some times in our lives. Finding the courage and imagination to face our problems is no easier for us than for these heroines of the Old Testament. Moses' mother's response was vital for the future of a nation. I am sure it was also heart-rending. The situations we face may demand equivalent courage and sacrifice. It is often so hard to know what to do, or how to find the strength to do it. How can we be wise?

We are back to the fear of the Lord again—for that, according to Psalm 111:10, is the beginning of wisdom.

A reminder: God grant me the serenity to accept the things I cannot change, the courage to change the things I can, and the wisdom to know the difference.

DA

Nile discovery

Pharaoh's daughter… saw the basket… She opened it and saw the baby. He was crying, and she felt sorry for him. 'This is one of the Hebrew babies,' she said.

Here we go again—God's plan for a whole nation being achieved through women. This time, a privileged young woman took pity on a helpless, doomed child. Pharaoh's daughter did not have to choose compassion: she could easily have ordered a servant to tip the basket into the river and gone back to painting her toenails. But no, it seems this lady had an inherited stubborn streak. Never mind that Daddy had a large political headache because of the Hebrews multiplying in his country. Never mind that in rescuing this Hebrew baby she was directly contradicting his orders. Her instinctive compassion was the overriding factor. Yet again, Pharaoh was to be outwitted by a determined woman who valued human life.

It is, of course, wonderfully ironic that Moses' mother was paid to nurse her own son, and that Moses was brought up with all the privileges of a princess's son, right under the nose of the enemy. He was even given an Egyptian name. Moses was being well grounded in the ways of the Egyptian court—knowledge he would draw on in his later vocation.

Sometimes it is impossible to see how God may be at work in situations, whether personal or political. The Israelites had to suffer and struggle in slavery for many more years before Moses came back to rescue them. But the plan was there, all the time, quietly growing in Pharaoh's own household, despite his futile attempts to quash God's people.

Next time you are tempted to think that God has forgotten you, or lost the plot somewhere, remember the story of Moses. God's timing or methods may not be the ones we would choose, but they are there nevertheless. Remember too, the privilege of being a woman. Without women, Moses never would have been.

'God is working his purpose out as year succeeds to year…'
ARTHUR CAMPBELL AINGER (1841–1919)
DA

Disaster!

*[Moses] saw an Egyptian beating a Hebrew, one of his own
people. Glancing this way and that and seeing no one, he killed
the Egyptian and hid him in the sand.*

It seems a shame that after all the heart-searching and risk-taking by the women in his life, Moses' first public action as an adult was a major disaster. Like them, he was moved by compassion, but unlike them, wisdom did not kick in when it should have done. His sense of outrage and longing for justice were good, but his impetuosity was not. Taking the law into his own hands was not going to work. Conscience-stricken, he hid the evidence in the sand. Within 24 hours, his action had become public knowledge. Fellow Hebrews were scathing rather than grateful—'Who made you ruler and judge over us?' (2:14)—and Pharaoh was after his blood. Moses had no choice but to go on the run.

It was not an auspicious start for the man who would one day lead the Hebrews to freedom. Now he was a murderer and a fugitive. Whatever his laudable motives in avenging his countryman, his hot-headed response had forfeited any chance of using his privileged position to help. Now he was in a worse situation than they were. What of his womenfolk? How his family must have despaired when he disappeared into the night! Heartbreak all round.

There is so much in this story that resonates with how life works out: high hopes dashed; loved ones making ghastly mistakes; impulsiveness for all the right reasons, leading to disaster. The passion that burned in Moses' heart for his fellow men now had nowhere to go. He could not fix it for them. The women, so faithful yet now deserted. The politics, continually unjust. The drama, unremitting.

I admire every single Hebrew who clung on to God in the midst of all this. Surely it must have seemed that God did not care. Isn't that the greatest challenge to our faith?

Read Habakkuk 3:16–19.

Dear Lord, help me to hang on in there with you. Amen.

                                        DA

A woman of grace

Moses... went to live in Midian, where he sat down by a well. Now a priest of Midian had seven daughters, and they came to draw water and fill the troughs to water their father's flock. Some shepherds came along and drove them away, but Moses got up and came to their rescue and watered their flock.

Guess who were the first people Moses met when he collapsed, exhausted by his escape, next to a well? Women, of course! Reuel's seven daughters had come to water their father's flock at the very same well. This turned out to be a wonderfully productive meeting, hinting at the grace of God. Moses had just lost everything and everyone. Now God gave him a new purpose and a new people. When other shepherds threatened the women, Moses' rescue mode took over and he piled in to help them. This time it was the right thing at the right time, and he ended up with invitations to dinner and marriage. Now he had a new woman in his life. She too turned out to be instrumental not only in bearing him children but in saving his life. Later, when God challenged Moses for not having circumcised his son, it was Zipporah who performed the deed so that God spared Moses' life (Exodus 4:24–26).

Israel may have been a patri-archal nation, but it was the women who made a difference in Moses' life at every turn, with ramifications for everyone. When life gets a bit wearing, keep in mind the story of Moses and how all these choices made by women added up to a dramatic story which foreshadows our own salvation. We only see a tiny part of the whole. Our individualistic Western society would have us believe that our decisions matter only to us. Don't be fooled. We all belong to God's great sweep of history, and we all have a vital part to play.

Read 1 Corinthians 12:12–31. Where do you fit?

DA

A bush experience

*Moses… came to Horeb, the mountain of God. There the angel of
the Lord appeared to him in flames of fire from within a bush.
Moses saw that though the bush was on fire it did not burn up.
So Moses thought, 'I will go over and see this strange sight—
why the bush does not burn up.'*

Here is another indelible picture
—Moses and the burning bush.
Moses had spent a good 40 years
learning his new life as husband,
father and shepherd in Midian
before the bush incident happened. His days revolved around
water, sheep and survival for his
family. Egypt was a regretful
memory. He was now a humble
shepherd, working with his
father-in-law's flocks. Then, one
day, the bush.

God was responding to his
people's cry, in his way and in
his time. As with other true
prophets in the Old Testament
(for example, Samuel and
Isaiah), Moses was called specifically. From the moment Moses
replied, 'Here I am' (3:4), his life
changed completely. Suddenly,
rescuing the Hebrews was back
on the agenda. But this time the
plan was massive. It was also to
be totally dependent on God.

How do we respond when
God calls us to do something,
however small or large? Moses
had been so well humbled by his
life's experiences that he was
reluctant and terrified. As a
compassionate God revealed to
him the rescue plan, Moses
wanted out. No more the hot-
headed activist, he asked God to
send someone else (4:13). This
man encountered God in flames
of fire in a bush, yet still he
resisted the call. This makes me
feel better about the many times
I argue with God about difficult
stuff. It's not that the absence of
burning bushes is a good excuse
for disobedience. But if a hero
like Moses struggled to accept
God's plan for his life, it does
help.

---

*Though he was angry at Moses'
reluctance, God did let him share
the burden with his older brother
Aaron. Whom do you depend
on? How about giving thanks for
them today?*

DA

Who are you, God?

*God said to Moses, 'I AM WHO I AM. This is what you are to say
to the Israelites: "I AM has sent me to you."' God also said to
Moses, 'Say to the Israelites, "The Lord, the God of your
fathers—the God of Abraham, the God of Isaac and the God of
Jacob—has sent me to you."'*

We are going to stick with Moses for a bit. At the beginning of a new year—and yes, we still are, even if routine has reasserted itself with a vengeance—he can encourage us. Despite the fact that he strides so powerfully through the most graphic pages of the Old Testament, his story is familiar. For he would have remained for ever in Midianite obscurity were it not for his burning encounter with God. Encounters with God do tend to change things.

Moses slowly came round to the idea that God thought he was the person for the job, despite his lack of confidence: 'Who am I, that I should go to Pharaoh?' (3:11). Gradually he realized that God was taking the initiative in the whole project. This was 'I AM' who was sending him and shouldering responsibility for the outcome.

Wrapped up in this seemingly enigmatic phrase is the most powerful promise that any of us ever need. God was not avoiding the question about his name. 'I AM' conveys a God who is always present with us, always existing, dynamically with us at all times. He is the Lord, or Yahweh, which literally means 'He is' or 'He will be'. He is not a new God—he identifies himself with Abraham, Isaac and Jacob, the God of the Hebrews. He is, always.

Tentatively, cautiously, Moses picks up his new role. Yet he knows he is not alone. How often do the tasks God sets us seem impossible? Again and again come the reassuring words, 'I will be with you' (3:12). I AM, the ever-present God, is there for us.

Read Exodus 3:1–14. How can today's encounter with God change you?

DA

Mission impossible

*Moses returned to the Lord and said, 'O Lord, why have you
brought trouble upon this people? Ever since I went to Pharaoh to
speak in your name, he has brought trouble upon this people, and
you have not rescued your people at all.'*

So Moses packed his bags, wife,
sons and donkey and set off for
Egypt. He took a wooden staff
and a growing conviction. He
met his big brother Aaron, and a
nation's emancipation began.

Together, the brothers gathered together the Israelite elders
and thrilled them with the news
of God's intervention. Moses
then marched into the courts
of his youth and demanded
the immediate release of the
Hebrews. Pharaoh was not im-
pressed and angrily increased
the Israelites' workload. Con-
demned to scavenging for straw
for brick-making, Moses' challenge had only increased the
Hebrew misery: 'May the Lord
look upon you and judge you!'
Thus the Israelite foremen
turned on Moses.

Despite the Disney-epic scale,
I can identify with the principles
here. Aren't there times when
we do what God has asked—it
takes all our determination—
and the situation deteriorates
forthwith? Or worse, those we
counted on for support turn

against us? Especially when it
comes from fellow Christians, I
think this is one of the hardest
experiences to bear.

Moses was merely encounter-
ing a reaction from his contem-
poraries which was to become
all too frequent in the wilderness years ahead. Few of us carry
comparable responsibility, but
most of us are let down by our
nearest and dearest at some
time. Did Moses stomp back
to Midian in disgust? No. He
took his pain where it belonged,
straight to his hotline to God.
God encouraged him and Moses
jumped back in, ready to face
Pharaoh and re-inspired to see
his people set free.

That has to be the right way
to deal with antagonism from
our compatriots. Take it to God
and let him set the agenda for
the future.

*'Forgive us our sins, for we also
forgive everyone who sins against
us…' (Luke 11:4).*

DA

Exodus 9:13b–14 (NIV)

The terrible ten

'This is what the Lord, the God of the Hebrews, says: Let my people go, so that they may worship me, or this time I will send the full force of my plagues against you and against your officials and your people, so you may know that there is no one like me in all the earth.'

Then there were the plagues. Again, this is awesomely visual stuff, irresistible to biblical illustrators and film-makers alike. Moses repeats his request, Pharaoh repeats his refusal, and God responds with another physical calamity. Moses' confidence in God's support grows and he becomes increasingly angry at Pharaoh's hard-heartedness. The Disney film *Prince of Egypt* explores the viable idea that Moses was squaring up to the playmate of his younger years. Certainly this feels like a very personal struggle.

From around the fourth plague, God differentiates between the Egyptians and Hebrews, sparing the latter. Blood, frogs, gnats, flies, livestock disease, boils, hail, locusts, darkness—natural phenomena under the command of God, bringing chaos to Egypt. By the plague of locusts, the court magicians are all out of magic, and the officials are begging Pharaoh to let the Israelites go.

Pharaoh tries bargaining: how about just the men? How about leaving your animals? But Moses will not budge. 'Hot with anger' (11:8), he storms out of the palace, having declared God's final judgment.

Had I been Moses, I might have been tempted to negotiate a little, especially if I was in conflict with an old playmate: 'OK, no hail if you let half the nation go. I'll clear up the boils if you let us go for two days instead of three.'

Moses endured ridicule, threats, sorcery and lies, but kept the target in his sights. I find it all too easy to lose sight of mine, and to doubt that God will back me up. Yet God has promised to give us everything we need (Ephesians 1:3) because he is always with us—he says so in his name. So whatever your Pharaoh is today, grab your staff and stand firm!

DA

The price of blood

*'On that same night I will pass through Egypt and strike down
every firstborn—both men and animals—and I will bring
judgment on all the gods of Egypt. I am the Lord. The blood will
be a sign for you on the houses where you are; and when I see the
blood, I will pass over you. No destructive plague will touch you
when I strike Egypt.'*

The big moment: Pharaoh has reached the end of the line and Moses the end of his tether. The scene is set for the Passover, the defining moment in Israel's history. A detailed ritual is instituted which is still enacted by Jews today, and which powerfully foreshadows Jesus' sacrifice on the cross. Only by the offering of a perfect lamb for each household could the Israelites escape the terrible judgment God would visit on the land—a life for a life. Only by the sign of blood on the doorposts would their firstborns be saved.

The instructions for this pre-exodus meal must have spread through the Israelite community like wildfire. A meal, yes, but special. Bitter herbs to represent their years of slavery. No yeast, no time. Pack up, we've got to be ready!

Every Israelite was to act as a priest for his family. No altar or public rite. An everyday activity sanctified by the greatest redemptive act in the Old Testament. Yet obedience was still vital. Lives were at stake.

Caught up in the moment, those first Passover participants had no idea of the incredible ramifications of their actions. Hundreds of years later, a young Jewish carpenter would transform this commemorative meal into something even more dynamic. God's amazing saving plan for the whole of humanity was swinging into action.

Pharaoh, meanwhile, had had enough. He called Moses and Aaron to the palace in the middle of the night, and begged them to leave with their nation. The exodus had begun…

---

*Dear Father, help me truly to
live in the new life that I have
because Jesus sacrificed himself
for me. Amen.*

DA

The way ahead

Moses answered the people, 'Do not be afraid. Stand firm and you will see the deliverance the Lord will bring you today. The Egyptians you see today you will never see again. The Lord will fight for you; you need only to be still.'

It happened! Moses led the people of Israel out of slavery in Egypt! God kept his promise. Laden with gifts, accompanied by non-Hebrews who presumably were Yahweh worshippers now, the nation moved out. Isn't it wonderful when we can clearly see God at work in a person's life, or in a situation, even in a country? It is so faith-invigorating! God is real! He does what he says he will do!'

Panic. 'What is that dust cloud following us? Is that really the Egyptian army? How can we escape them across the Red Sea? Moses, how could you do this to us? We're doomed, and we're going to die!'

Poor Moses, loved and hated within the space of hours. Thus rushes the rollercoaster of life—up to the heights and down to the depths. No sooner is one battle won than a new challenge comes along.

Let Moses be an encouragement to you. He has seen enough now to know that God will not let him down. His impassioned speech applies to us too. We too can choose to 'stand firm' in the threatening crises of life and trust God for the outcome. It is not easy. There must have been many terrified people clustered by the water that day. But God, and Moses, understood their fear and encouraged them to trust. How Moses has changed since that first nervous desert encounter with God! Now his words reverberate down the centuries and speak to us too.

We all have the potential, like Moses, to grow in our understanding of and trust in God. Unlike Moses, however, we do not have to save ourselves or anyone else. Jesus has done that for us. Enjoy!

God saved Israel by parting the Red Sea and drowning the Egyptians. What is his way ahead for you?

DA

Genesis 2:7, 18, 21–25 (NRSV)

Not alone

The Lord God said, 'It is not good that the man should be alone.'

Samuel, a former elder of our church, has recently returned to his home country of Tanzania to make contact with a group of five hundred Tanzanian Christians who have come together in the village where Samuel's family originated, with the desire of starting a church. Samuel hopes to minister to this community of believers.

For the next few days, we are going to look at the local church as a community—a concept that perhaps many Christians and many churches have lost sight of in our day and age, and possibly more particularly in our Western culture. We tend to be so very individualistic. Many people choose to live alone. Others have no choice in the matter and are just plain lonely.

However, that is not how God intended it to be. Having created man in his own image, God said it was not 'good' that he should be alone, so he created another human being—woman—to come to his rescue, to be one with him. This is the beginning of community, of togetherness, which reflects the oneness clearly existing already from all time within the three Persons of the Trinity. 'Community is deeply grounded in the nature of God... Therefore the making of community may not be regarded as an optional decision for Christians' (Gilbert Bilezikian, *Community 101*).

We shall learn, through the passages of scripture we shall be studying together, God's purpose for the local church and how we can live out more fully in practice this fundamental teaching about community, explained and illustrated in a variety of ways in the Bible.

Lord, open our eyes as we look into your word. Help us to grasp and understand your teaching about the church. Show us the importance of being part of a body of believers, and reveal to us the part you want us to play within the church where you have placed us.

BA

23

Amazing grace

I give thanks to my God always for you because of the grace of God that has been given you in Christ Jesus.

In October 2000 our church embarked upon a study of 1 Corinthians. Twice a year, we are accustomed to do what we call an 'integrated Bible study'. During however many weeks the study lasts, personal study, group study and Sunday sermons all centre on the same topic or passage of scripture. Our fellowship Bible study groups are good ways to encourage the sense of community, as people get to know one another more easily in a small group and generally feel comfortable sharing.

1 Corinthians was rather a daunting study to begin, because of the many problems reflected in the church in Corinth, which the apostle Paul deals with in this letter. It struck me, in the light of all these difficulties, that the opening words of the apostle Paul are most encouraging. In spite of their imperfections, these Christians formed the body of Christ; they had been set apart for God; they were beneficiaries of his grace, and lacked no spiritual gift. And what's more, they would be 'blameless on the day of our Lord Jesus Christ' (v. 8). We wonder how that could be when we read of divisions within the church, of immorality, of lawsuits among the members, and many other problems. It is certainly not through their own efforts that they would become blameless. It is due to God's grace and faithfulness. 'God is faithful; by him you were called into the fellowship of his Son, Jesus Christ our Lord' (v. 9). God called them, and he will not abandon them. He will see them through to the end of time and for all eternity. When we look at our own churches, we see imperfections and problems; we see divisions and sin. But God is still faithful.

Lord, we praise you for your faithfulness, and for the work you are doing within us to make us like Jesus so that we might be blameless on that day.

BA

TUESDAY 15 JANUARY   *1 Corinthians 12:12–27 (NRSV)*

Great is your faithfulness

You are the body of Christ and individually members of it.

'We are the body of Christ.' So sang a small group of members of our church in Geneva on the occasion of its 30th anniversary. For the thirty years of its existence, this church has grouped members of many different nationalities and cultures. Being an English-language congregation in a French-speaking city, the turnover tends to be fairly rapid, as people are relocated to jobs in Geneva for a relatively short time before moving on elsewhere. So it was particularly heart-warming to see the number of former members who came back for our special weekend of celebration and thanksgiving. They came from Korea, South Africa, Lebanon, USA, Holland, UK and other parts of Switzerland to celebrate God's faithfulness.

Jim and Charlene had not been back to Geneva since returning to the USA in the 1970s. Converted soon after their arrival at the church, through the quiet, consistent testimony of a fellow American, they have gone on to serve God in their own country. 'We can't even begin to tell you what this trip has meant to us,' they exclaimed, as they once again found themselves in Geneva, gathered with their brothers and sisters in Christ from around the world.

Florence too was back. Now 80 years old, she testified to the fact that 'in 1968 I was a jaded, worn-out person with a life that was a disaster, but because of people who became the nucleus of this church, and their loving-kindness and their caring' she and her children all became Christians.

As we concluded our service that Sunday by singing 'Great is thy faithfulness', I looked around the greatly increased congregation. As all these people from different periods of the church's history stood together to sing God's praises, once again I thought, 'What a foretaste of heaven!'

'The steadfast love of the Lord never ceases, his mercies never come to an end; they are new every morning; great is your faithfulness' (Lamentations 3:22–23).
BA

25

Belonging

We, who are many, are one body in Christ, and individually we are members one of another.

Our church in Geneva tends to be a rather transient 'body', as members come and go. So, in order to encourage people to get involved in the church and to help them discern their gifts, a list of church activities and areas of service has been drawn up. Once a year, we are encouraged 'not to think of [ourselves] more highly than [we] ought to think, but to think with sober judgment, each according to the measure of faith that God has assigned' (v. 3) and to see where we can most effectively use our God-given gifts in service through the church. The list is not exhaustive, leaving open the possibilities for new ministries to develop according to the gifts represented in the church at the time. 'Each one should use whatever gift he has received to serve others' (1 Peter 4:10, NIV).

Here in our passage today, Paul uses the human body as an illustration of the church. This is true community—working together, serving together, suffering together, rejoicing together. 'Togetherness' was a characteristic of the early church right from the beginning. In Acts 2 we read, 'When the day of Pentecost came, they were all *together* in one place... All the believers were *together* and had everything in common... Every day they continued to meet *together* in the temple courts. They broke bread in their homes and ate *together* with glad and sincere hearts' (Acts 2:1, 44, 46, NIV).

God did not intend us to live in isolation. We are meant to be in relationship with one another. We are brothers and sisters in Christ, members of the same family, parts of the same body. We need to function as such.

'We must grow up in every way into him who is the head, into Christ, from whom the whole body, joined and knit together by every ligament with which it is equipped, as each part is working properly, promotes the body's growth in building itself up in love' (Ephesians 4:15–16).

BA

Rejoicing and weeping

Rejoice with those who rejoice, weep with those who weep.

Three of the phone calls I had today from members of our church stood out to me as significant for a number of reasons, and not least in relation to the theme of these notes, the church as community.

Nana, a Ghanaian member, phoned this morning, rejoicing and praising the Lord because she has successfully defended her thesis and is now 'by the grace of God, a qualified social worker'. Her thesis was exceptionally well received by the examiners, who praised her for her excellent work. Nana, who knew that the church had been praying, felt supported and upheld throughout the ordeal and phoned to share the good news and to thank us for our prayers. She remarked how precious it was to be part of the body of Christ.

In the evening, another member phoned to say that she has just been diagnosed with cancer, already in an advanced stage, which has metastasized into the brain. With no family of her own, she counts on the love and care and support of the church family.

The final phone call of the day was from Apollo, a Chinese Christian, to announce that his wife has just given birth to their second child. Their joy was increased by the fact that their baby boy was delivered by Annie, a Scottish midwife, also a member of our church, thus keeping it all in the family!

Yes, we are to 'rejoice with those who rejoice, and weep with those who weep' (v. 15). This is true 'body life'. 'If one member suffers, all suffer together with it; if one member is honoured, all rejoice together with it' (1 Corinthians 12:26). We rejoice with Nana and with Apollo and his family at their good news. We 'suffer' with Esther and will continue to uphold her in prayer in the days to come, and seek to be a comfort and an encouragement to her.

'Bear one another's burdens, and in this way you will fulfil the law of Christ' (Galatians 6:2).

BA

Harmony

Live in harmony with one another.

If the apostle Paul thought it necessary to exhort the members of the church in Rome to 'live in harmony with one another', it was obviously for a reason. Human nature being what it is, harmonious relationships have to be worked at; they don't just happen. The remainder of this verse suggests that some of the people in that church considered themselves superior to others: they were too 'haughty' to associate with the more 'lowly' members. To the Philippian believers Paul writes, 'In humility regard others as better than yourselves' (Philippians 2:3) and he encourages them to be like Jesus, 'who, though he was in the form of God… emptied himself, taking the form of a slave, being born in human likeness. And… he humbled himself and became obedient to the point of death—even death on a cross' (Philippians 2:6–8). Paul mentions by name two women in that church who were having trouble agreeing. 'I urge Euodia and Syntyche,' he writes, 'to be of the same mind in the Lord' (Philippians 4:2).

It is very easy to focus on causes of irritation and annoyance rather than on the Lord. A church such as ours, with members from all over the world, representing widely varying cultures and customs, is asking for trouble! In practice, however, what could have been divisive has in fact been tremendously enriching—which is not to say that we never have any problems and misunderstandings.

Sushila, a former member, now back in India, wrote at the time of our 30th anniversary that it was here she had 'understood the real meaning of unity in diversity. People from all the four corners of the world and from all walks of life saw eye to eye because their gaze was fixed on Jesus, the author and finisher of our faith'. If only we could *always* keep our eyes fixed on him!

Lord, forgive our arrogance and pride. Help us truly to consider others as better than ourselves and to keep our eyes fixed on Jesus.

BA

Forgiveness

Then Peter came and said to him, 'Lord, if another member of the church sins against me, how often should I forgive? As many as seven times?' Jesus said to him, 'Not seven times, but, I tell you, seventy-seven times.'

How often do we hear on the news, or even in the street, and all around us, of conflict, hatred and a desire for revenge? If evil is done to you, then retaliate by giving as good as you get. Stand up for your rights. Your honour is at stake. We seem to have an acute sense of justice—especially when we are personally wronged—and we are quick to retaliate and condemn.

Nowhere, I think, is the Christian message so radically opposed to the way of 'the world' than in the area of forgiveness. 'See that none of you repays evil for evil, but always seek to do good to one another and to all,' writes the apostle Paul (1 Thessalonians 5:15). 'Love your enemies,' says Jesus (Matthew 5:44), and Paul adds, 'If your enemies are hungry, feed them; if they are thirsty, give them something to drink' (Romans 12:20).

In his reply to Peter, the Lord makes it clear that we must forgive not once, or twice, or even seven times, but repeatedly. It is only as we realize how much God has forgiven us that we in turn will be able to forgive others. It is a well-known fact that those who harbour a spirit of hatred and revenge in their heart are the ones who will suffer most as these negative emotions begin to fester. So, for our own good, as well as for harmony within the body, forgiveness is to be characteristic of the Christian.

Jesus teaches that the forgiveness we receive from God is conditional on the forgiveness we offer to others: 'For if you forgive others their trespasses, your heavenly Father will also forgive you; but if you do not forgive others, neither will your Father forgive your trespasses' (Matthew 6:14–15).

BA

Living stones

Like living stones, let yourselves be built into a spiritual house.

Soon after the 30th anniversary celebrations of our church, my husband and I left for the USA to visit other former members in Minnesota, North and South Carolina, and Maryland, some of the 'living stones' who had gone to make up the building whose 'foundation is Jesus Christ' (1 Corinthians 3:11). We had been intrigued to learn, some months earlier, that business had drawn together Scott from North Carolina, and Charlie from South Carolina, and caused them to discover, with surprised delight, that they had both been a part of our church family in Geneva at different times of its history, about twenty years apart!

In Maryland, we enjoyed another happy time of reunion when our hosts invited other past members of our church family from the surrounding area, mainly Americans, but one British couple and a girl from Sierra Leone. Some of them already knew each other, as their time in Geneva had overlapped, but others met for the first time on that joyful occasion. Members of different churches now, we remain united by our common faith in Jesus Christ; all children of the same Father, with the same lifeblood coursing through our veins; all bound together with love; all committed to following Jesus.

The picture of the building is only one illustration used by Paul in chapter 3 of his first letter to the Corinthians, along with that of the field and that of the temple. Addressing this church, where there are divisions, immorality, and many other problems, he makes the following amazing statement: 'Do you not know that you are God's temple and that God's Spirit dwells in you?' (1 Corinthians 3:16). Imperfect as our churches may be, that is where God has chosen to dwell by his Spirit and that is where he is going to be manifest today.

'God's temple is holy, and you are that temple,' continues Paul at the end of 1 Corinthians 3:17. What, then, are the implications for us in terms of holy living?

BA

God's people

You are a chosen race, a royal priesthood, a holy nation, God's own people.

Here we have four expressions illustrating the church as community: 'a chosen race, a royal priesthood, a holy nation, God's own people'. Modern usage of the word 'church' can often lead to misunderstanding. In many cases, it has come to refer to the building where Christians meet for worship, rather than to the people worshipping there. Hence we talk about 'going to church', when in actual fact, together as believers in Jesus Christ, we *are* the church. As 'priests' we are to 'offer spiritual sacrifices acceptable to God through Jesus Christ' (1 Peter 2:5) as we worship him and minister to one another. As God's people, we are to be holy in all our conduct (see 1 Peter 1:15–16).

Nancy, from Lebanon, writing after our anniversary weekend, remarked that ours 'is a church that shouldn't work— with a changing congregation and people from different cultures, denominations, economic situations. How is it that they do so well at getting along?' She concluded that it is due to 'the honour given to the Lord'.

Douglas, another of our former members, stressed how important it is that people be made to feel welcome when they first come along to a service. This initial contact can often turn into an invitation to a meal and then perhaps to a Bible study group. This kind of sharing is unfortunately not characteristic of all the churches he has visited since leaving Switzerland. He pointed out that in many churches people are 'just attenders'. Writing to the Christians in Ephesus, Paul says, 'You are no longer strangers and aliens, but you are citizens with the saints and also members of the household of God' (Ephesians 2:19).

Let us determine, in so far as it depends on us, to be welcoming to newcomers to our church, so that they will quickly feel themselves to be 'members of the household of God' and no longer 'strangers and aliens'.

BA

Entertaining angels?

Be hospitable to one another without complaining.

Being in a multi-cultural church implies very often eating multi-cultural meals—Chinese, Indian, French, Ghanaian, Eritrean, Italian, and so on… even English!—an activity that most of us thoroughly enjoy. On a Sunday, after the service, when everyone is invited to partake, or in smaller groups in homes, or on the occasion of 'international evenings', there are many opportunities for extending hospitality. Church members often open their homes to offer accommodation to those passing through the Geneva area. Arising from this, some years ago we ran a column in our magazine entitled 'Feasting in fellowship', where members contributed recipes from their home country. These recipes were later compiled into our own church cookbook! The editor wrote in the foreword, 'The overall purpose of this book is to encourage you to show hospitality to one another.'

Having frequently benefited, particularly during my student days, from the hospitality of others (in fact, it was in the home of missionaries in France that I first met my husband), I realize what a good way this is to get alongside people and show love to them. At one stage of our ministry, our home was filled each week with unchurched, hungry French teenagers, who shared our meal before we opened up the word of God to them. Peter tells us to do this 'without complaining'. True, it can be hard work, but it is well worth it, so let us do it ungrudgingly. Surely part of living out the reality of the body of Christ is to invite members into our homes. Hospitality is a great way of deepening fellowship and contributing to the body life of the church. And, through offering hospitality to strangers, who knows but that you may have 'entertained angels without knowing it' (Hebrews 13:2)!

Thank you, Lord, for all those who have offered hospitality to us. Thank you too for the homes you have given us. Show us how best to use them for you.

BA

Servants

*'If I, your Lord and Teacher, have washed your feet, you also
ought to wash one another's feet.'*

Bill, a top executive and successful businessman, became
part of our church. After a fellowship meal or other activity,
whom would we see sweeping
the hall or cleaning up? Yes,
you've guessed—Bill. Because of
his humility and consistency
and because, as one person who
was converted through Bill's testimony put it, 'he lived out
Monday through Saturday what
he was on Sunday', people were
drawn to Jesus.

In our passage today, we have
a supreme example of service
and servanthood shown to the
early disciples and to us by our
'Lord and Teacher', the Son of
God himself. This humble act of
service leaves no room for pride
or hierarchy. Why didn't one of
the disciples perform the traditional foot-washing? Probably
because they all expected a servant to do it—which would
have been customary. But no
servant appeared. Even if it
didn't occur to them to wash
each other's feet, couldn't one
of them at least have washed the
feet of their Master? But no, it is
the Master himself who gets up,
takes off his outer garment, puts
a towel round himself, fills a
bowl with water and begins to
wash and dry the feet of men
who thought themselves above
such a menial task. What an
impact this visual aid must have
had upon them! What an acted-
out lesson in humility and servanthood! And, as if that
weren't clear enough, just in
case they haven't yet got the
message, Jesus states explicitly,
'You ought to wash one
another's feet. For I have set you
an example, that you also
should do as I have done to you'
(vv. 14b–15).

---

*Lord, forgive our selfishness and
pride. Help us to follow your
example to 'serve one another in
love' (Galatians 5:13, NIV).*

BA

Love

> *'This is my commandment, that you love one another
> as I have loved you.'*

Many years ago, in the early 1970s, the years during which our children were being born, we lived in an apartment block in France, near the Swiss border. People from the church would come across with meals, offers of help and gifts for the children. One of our neighbours had obviously noticed what was going on and, amazed, remarked to me on the love that was being shown by our Christian friends. Probably many of us have benefited from the love of our brothers and sisters in Christ in many practical ways—a meal in times of illness, transportation, babysitting… There are many ways of expressing love in action. Laura, one of our church members, some years ago had to go to the hospital every day for radiotherapy. We took it in turns to drive her there. One day the nurse remarked on all these different people who accompanied her. 'Oh, they are all my brothers and sisters!' said Laura.

'Love one another deeply from the heart,' writes the apostle Peter (1 Peter 1:22). Love should be such a striking char-

acteristic of the church that Paul writes about it repeatedly in his letters; James exhorts his readers to show love in very practical ways; Peter picks up on the theme, and it is a recurring subject in John's letters. Add to that the very specific teaching by Jesus about love and we are obliged to acknowledge the importance of it.

In fact, our love for one another is proof of our love for the Lord. 'Just as I have loved you,' says Jesus, 'you also should love one another. By this everyone will know that you are my disciples, if you have love for one another' (John 13:34b–35). Writing to the Thessalonians, Paul acknowledges the fact that they love 'all the brothers and sisters throughout Macedonia', but he urges them 'to do so more and more'.

Let us love one another, more and more!

BA

The church at prayer

While Peter was kept in prison, the church prayed fervently to God for him.

We often think of prayer as a private, personal occupation. And so it must be, of course, but not exclusively so, and not always. We certainly need to spend time alone with God in prayer. However, as we have mentioned more than once already in these notes, the Christian life is not meant to be lived out in isolation, but in the fellowship of other believers. We have a special promise from Jesus concerning our meeting together to pray: 'If two of you agree on earth about anything you ask, it will be done for you by my Father in heaven. For where two or three are gathered in my name, I am there among them' (Matthew 18:19–20).

In our passage today we see a church at prayer. 'While Peter was kept in prison, the church prayed fervently for him' (v. 5). These prayers were effective, and God answered. 'The Lord has sent his angel and rescued me,' realized Peter, when he eventually 'came to himself' (v. 11). Immediately he went 'to the house of Mary, the mother of John whose other name was Mark, where many had gathered and were praying' (v. 12). They were 'overjoyed' (v. 14) and 'amazed' (v. 16), and Peter 'described for them how the Lord had brought him out of the prison' (v. 17). What a tremendous answer to prayer!

I wonder how many gather for prayer meetings in your church? What an immense privilege to be able to meet together in the Lord's name, knowing that he is present in our midst, and to bring before him people who need his touch upon their lives, and situations which he is powerful to transform.

The apostle Paul encourages the church at Ephesus to 'always keep on praying for all the saints' (Ephesians 6:18, NIV), and James writes in his letter, 'Pray for one another' (James 5:16). Let us do just that! And, praise God when he answers!

BA

One another

Encourage one another and build up each other… Always seek to do good to one another.

It is amazing how often the little phrase 'one another' appears in the scripture passages that these notes are based upon. 'Love one another'; 'live in harmony with one another'; 'be hospitable to one another'; 'wash one another's feet'; 'bear one another's burdens'; 'forgive one another'; 'pray for one another'; 'encourage one another'; 'do good to one another'. If there were any evidence needed that an isolated Christian is an anomaly, and that we are meant to be in relationship, I think we have it in these two words repeated over and over again in the New Testament.

What wonderful churches we would have if we all lived out to the full these various exhortations! Maybe we should start taking them seriously, and put them into practice. Love, service, hospitality, prayer, forgiveness, burden-bearing, doing good, encouragement, will result in harmonious relationships and a healthy body with all the members working well together and functioning as God intended.

The world can be a hard place to live in, and we are easily subject to many kinds of fears. In the light of this, and in contrast to it, the church is to be a place where believers are to encourage one another, build each other up and do good to one another. We can do this in a variety of ways, through drawing alongside in sympathy, through offering practical help, through our prayers. Paul's focus in this passage, however, is on the glorious truth that Christ is coming back and 'we will be with the Lord for ever' (4:17). We can build each other up and encourage one another most of all by reminding one another of this great truth.

Lord, thank you for my brothers and sisters in Christ. Help us to put into practice the exhortations in your word, so that your body will function as you intended. May we always seek to do good to one another.

BA

Paul's overriding passion

After this Paul left Athens and went to Corinth. There he found a Jew named Aquila, a native of Pontus, who had recently come from Italy with his wife Priscilla, because Claudius had ordered all Jews to leave Rome.

Paul was still on the move. He sailed westward from Athens to the bustling, cosmopolitan city of Corinth, perfectly situated to control trade on the narrow stretch of land between the Aegean and Adriatic Seas. Here, all nationalities mingled and gathered in a dramatic setting, dominated by the great temple of Aphrodite, the goddess of love. By the time Paul arrived, probably in AD50, Corinth was already infamous for its thousands of temple prostitutes and general excess and debauchery—hardly a promising place in which to try to capture people's attention with the gospel!

Paul didn't waste any time. Soon he was speaking in the local synagogue, arguing, as he had done in so many different places before, about the significance of the life, death and resurrection of Jesus Christ. Paul also very quickly met up with some fellow Jews who had recently moved to Corinth from Rome, and, because of a shared profession, either tentmaking or leatherworking, Paul was invited to live with them. This is the first time we are introduced to Aquila and Priscilla, two strangers who were to become some of Paul's closest friends and fellow workers in the faith.

As Paul travelled around, we sense his unflagging determination to tell others about Christ, and a hungry impatience to meet with and talk to as many people as possible. We also see that wherever he went, he identified and taught people who would become the leaders of the local church, spending hours and days with them, pouring into them all he could of his vision and understanding of his beloved Lord.

Dear Lord, please help us to see you so clearly that we become alight with the same fire that burned in Paul. Amen.

Read 1 Corinthians 2.

CR

A reassuring word

When they opposed and reviled him, in protest he shook the dust from his clothes and said to them, 'Your blood be on your own heads! I am innocent. From now on I will go to the Gentiles.'

It had all started so well! Paul had settled into life in Corinth with new friends and his customary vigour and drive. Both Jews and Greeks were coming to faith after hearing him preach. However, at some point things started to turn sour.

Two of Paul's trusty co-workers, Silas and Timothy, had also joined him in Corinth, but by then some of the Jews who did not accept Jesus as the promised Messiah had begun to turn nasty. Paul realized the strength of their opposition, and he must have sensed his life was in danger.

Instead of giving up on preaching or lying low for a while, Paul promptly shifted his focus to the Gentile population, and carried on—with amazing results. More and more people believed in Christ and were baptized. It is at this point that Luke records a vision Paul had one night, in which the Lord encouraged Paul not to be afraid and to keep on speaking out.

What Luke does not record, and what we can only imagine, are the anxious conversations between Paul and his friends, and Paul's own fears. It's easy to see Paul as a superhuman hero, a bit fiery and reactionary, but basically unaffected by all the opposition. The reality was probably that he felt very frightened and vulnerable. Why else would Jesus have spoken to him with such words of solidarity and reassurance, comfort and encouragement? Paul's courage was revived, and he continued preaching in Corinth for a further year and a half.

Lord, sometimes I get frightened and discouraged. Through your Holy Spirit please speak the words I need to hear. Amen.

CR

An unusual helping hand

Just as Paul was about to speak, Gallio said to the Jews, 'If it were a matter of crime or serious villainy, I would be justified in accepting the complaint of you Jews; but since it is a matter of questions about words and names and your own law, see to it yourselves; I do not wish to be a judge of these matters.'

Paul had been hauled before a high official, the proconsul of Achaia. He was about to take a deep breath and launch into a defence of his message when Gallio, the proconsul, made a surprise decision: he told the Jews to sort out their problems with Paul themselves. By doing so, he implied that Paul's message was in theory as valid as other forms of Judaism.

From then on, Christian teaching would be recognized, at least officially, as being entitled to the same standing as other strands of Jewish teaching. The group of men who had taken Paul to Gallio were not pleased. They realized they couldn't touch Paul, so they took out their anger by beating up the poor leader of the synagogue instead!

Paul was well accustomed to defending himself, and it must have been a strange and pleasant surprise to realize that, for once, someone else was arguing his case, albeit in a different way than he would have done.

Sometimes I quote the old cliché, 'God works in mysterious ways', and I believe that God's Holy Spirit is quite capable of transforming people and circumstances. All too often, however, I behave as if God is not at work, and as if the outcome rests entirely on my shoulders. I plan and pray, which is right and proper, but I also worry and fret and second-guess and 'what-if'. In short, as well as doing my part, I try to do God's too!

Dear Lord, help me to trust you with all that is on my mind and heart. Amen.

Read Psalm 121.

CR

Who's got you?

When he had landed at Caesarea, he went up to Jerusalem and greeted the church, and then went down to Antioch. After spending some time there he departed and went from place to place through the region of Galatia and Phrygia, strengthening all the disciples.

There is a wonderful scene in the first of the *Superman* films starring Christopher Reeves, when Superman swoops through the air and catches Lois Lane as she is falling to the ground. 'Don't worry,' he says reassuringly as he rescues her, 'I've got you!' She stares at him with a mixture of wonder and disbelief: 'You've got me,' she shrieks, 'but who's got you?'

Paul is on the move again, sailing from city to city, revisiting the churches he had established on his earlier journeys. Just reading about his itinerary and activities is exhausting, yet Luke comments that everywhere Paul went, he spent his time preaching, arguing for the truth of the Christian message and strengthening the disciples.

We know that Paul was a man with a special mission, and we also know that he was only human; yet he kept up a pace and a programme that seems more suited to a superhero. What was his secret? What was he running on?

From what we can learn of Paul through his many letters, we discover a man who kept his eyes on Jesus and who was continually aware of the miracle of his salvation, freedom and new life in Christ. We also know that he drew on the strength and comfort of the Holy Spirit. Paul could do what he did because he stayed connected to the source of all his vision and power.

Dear Lord, please keep us close and connected to you. When we feel weary, distant or alone, help us to remember that you are always there to fill us with new hope and strength and joy. Amen.

Read John 15:5 and 2 Corinthians 5:14–15.

CR

Helping or hindering?

He began to speak boldly in the synagogue; but when Priscilla and Aquila heard him, they took him aside and explained the Way of God to him more accurately.

Paul had left his good friends Priscilla and Aquila in Ephesus as he carried on with his missionary journeys. While they were there, Apollos, a Jewish scholar from Alexandria, along with a small group of companions, came to visit Ephesus on the way to Corinth. Apollos was highly educated and had an eloquent and compelling style of teaching. Part of his message was that the baptism of John was indeed in keeping with the Jewish tradition. Priscilla and Aquila instantly realized that Apollos knew a great deal about the story of Jesus, but that he had not fully grasped the purpose and meaning of the gospel.

What Priscilla and Aquila did next should be a lesson on how we are to respond to other Christians and to those who are seeking after truth. Instead of listening to Apollos and then criticizing him for what he did *not* know, the wise couple took him aside and explained how the baptism of John was pointing to an acceptance of Jesus as the Messiah, with a new type of baptism in the name of Christ.

Apollos responded enthusiastically to their teaching and immediately acknowledged the significance of Jesus. Priscilla and Aquila encouraged him to visit the newly founded Christian community when he got to Corinth, and they also sent a letter to the Christians there, commending Apollos to them.

If Priscilla and Aquila had not taken the time and trouble to talk to Apollos, or if they had spoken out against him and damaged his reputation, he might never have learned the truth of Christ and been able to preach the full gospel. As it was, Apollos later became the leader of the church at Corinth, and eventually he became its first bishop.

Dear Lord, help us always to encourage and build up others, for the sake of your kingdom. Amen

Read 1 Corinthians 3:1–23.

CR

Into what, then, were you baptized?

He said to them, 'Did you receive the Holy Spirit when you became believers?' They replied, 'No, we have not even heard that there is a Holy Spirit.'

Paul had arrived at Ephesus, which, like Corinth, was another great commercial city. Ephesus was seen as the place where east met west, with its accompanying mix of cultures and lifestyles. Just as Corinth was dominated by the temple of Aphrodite, Ephesus was the centre of the worship of Artemis, who was the equivalent of the Roman goddess Diana. At the time Paul was visiting Ephesus, the magnificent temple of Artemis was considered to be one of the seven wonders of the world.

Paul quickly met up with a small group of believers. As he asked them about their faith, he learned that they were in fact disciples of John the Baptist. Paul explained that John's baptism had to do with repentance, and that John had been trying to prepare people for the baptism that Jesus would offer. Being baptized in the name of Jesus was to receive God's Holy Spirit, and these Ephesians had never even heard of the Holy Spirit!

However, they accepted Paul's teaching and were duly baptized in the name of Jesus. When Paul laid his hands on them, they received the Holy Spirit and immediately manifested some of the gifts of the Spirit, such as speaking in tongues and prophesying.

It is sad to think that there is still confusion and disagreement among Christians today about exactly what it means to be baptized in the name of Jesus and what is the role of the Holy Spirit. For Paul, being baptized was to receive the fullness of God's Spirit, and such a gift was intended to be life-changing! How else could Jesus' followers be transformed themselves and carry on his transforming work?

Loving Lord, please fill me with your Spirit and make me willing to receive all that you want to give me. Amen.

Read John 1:29–34 and Acts 1:1–8.

CR

Arguing and pleading

He entered the synagogue and for three months spoke out boldly,
and argued persuasively about the kingdom of God.

Except for politicians, lawyers and campaigners, we're not really accustomed to hearing people arguing their point of view. The worthy principles of balance and tolerance seem to rule in every arena, and society's underlying drift towards relativism makes arguing passionately for a set of beliefs almost embarrassing. After all, who wants to come across as a blinkered fanatic?

Paul didn't seem to care about how he came across, as long as he was preaching the good news of Jesus Christ. Some translations of today's verse speak of Paul pleading as well as arguing. We gain a picture of the great disciple grappling vigorously with every objection and counterargument that was thrown at him, and going beyond that to plead, beg and urge his audience to accept Jesus as the promised Messiah.

The thought of Paul, in common with many people today, shrugging his shoulders and saying that, at the end of the day, it really didn't matter what they believed, as long as their beliefs didn't hurt anybody, seems laughable. For him, it mattered so much that, ultimately, he was willing to put his own life on the line.

We may be annoyed at the rampant relativism we encounter, but in a sense we are fortunate that in our country a wide range of beliefs is tolerated. In many places around the world, Christians and those of other faiths are being put to death because of what they believe. But if we do believe we have been introduced to the one who is the Way, the Truth and the Life, what are we doing so that others might know Christ?

Lord of mercy and truth, help us to know when and how to speak out in the name of Christ. Help us also to know that it is usually our actions that speak louder than our words. Amen.

Read 1 Corinthians 9:15–27.

CR

Battling evil

Also many of those who became believers confessed and disclosed their practices. A number of those who practised magic collected their books and burned them publicly; when the value of these books was calculated, it was found to come to fifty thousand silver coins. So the word of the Lord grew mightily and prevailed.

Besides being the centre for worshipping Artemis, Ephesus was known for its fascination with the magic arts. The Ephesians sold so many papyrus scrolls of magic spells that these books became known as 'Ephesian letters'.

It was in this context that Paul went about, preaching and teaching the good news of Jesus Christ. But that's not all he did: Luke tells us that Paul's power was such that when pieces of cloth that he had touched were taken to the sick, people were healed of their diseases and evil spirits left them.

It wasn't long before some of the local Jewish exorcists heard of what Paul was doing, and thought they'd have a go at casting out evil spirits in the name of Jesus. However, their attempts backfired rather spectacularly, and people began to be aware of something different about Paul and the God in whose name he ministered.

They learned that it was through the power of the Holy Spirit and in the name of Jesus that Paul was able to perform healings, miracles and exorcisms. Many people repented of their occult practices and brought their books of magic spells to Paul to be burned.

Today we still come up against forces that would draw people away from the light and truth of Christ into the darkness and lies of evil, and we still have to pray for God's power and protection, wisdom and discernment. Although we encounter evil in this world, through Jesus' death and resurrection we can be certain that evil does not have ultimate power.

Dear Lord, keep our eyes and our hearts fixed on you, and help us to bring others into your healing and life-giving light. Amen.

CR

Acts 19:21–41 (NRSV)

Making an impact

A man named Demetrius, a silversmith who made silver shrines of Artemis, brought no little business to the artisans. These he gathered together, with the workers of the same trade, and said, 'Men, you know that we get our wealth from this business. You also see and hear that not only in Ephesus but in almost the whole of Asia this Paul has persuaded and drawn away a considerable number of people by saying that gods made with hands are not gods.'

Paul was really stirring up trouble in Ephesus! Not only had he ruined business for a number of local exorcists, now, as a result of his preaching, he was threatening the livelihood of the silversmiths. How extraordinary to think that the effect Paul was having on the Ephesians was beginning to extend to their traditional rituals and practices. It's as if a preacher in Soho was affecting the buying habits of those who patronized the local porn shops. No wonder the merchants were upset!

One of the silversmiths managed to whip his colleagues and unsuspecting members of the public into an unruly crowd. Once again, Paul and his friends were saved by the intervention of a civic official, a man named Alexander, who argued that the newcomers were not breaking any laws, and that it was the people in the crowd who were in danger of being charged with rioting.

Paul was saved from the mob, but he realized it would be unsafe to preach openly any longer in Ephesus. Soon he would be on the move again, but he would leave Ephesus buzzing with stories of what he had said and done, with many people having had their lives and faith profoundly challenged by the message of the gospel.

Thank you Lord, for Paul's obedience, courage and faith, and for his willingness to challenge the beliefs and practices of the people he met. Amen.

CR

Just names?

He was accompanied by Sopater son of Pyrrhus from Beroea, by Aristarchus and Secundus from Thessalonica, by Gaius from Derbe, and by Timothy, as well as by Tychicus and Trophimus from Asia.

If you are anything like me, you've probably glanced at the verse for today and not even attempted to pronounce all the unfamiliar names! As I typed out the verse, my word processor underlined just about every other word with a wiggly red line, indicating either lots of misspellings or unknown words.

It's easy to concentrate on Paul and what he did, forgetting that as he travelled around he continually taught and trained many new Christians to carry on the work of spreading the gospel.

Some leaders are naturally gifted at mentoring others and 'growing their successors'. For Paul, who was clearly an excellent teacher, it was not an option but a necessity. He knew that if other believers were not equipped and enabled to teach the faith, the message of Christ would not be preached.

We will never know the stories of all the men and women who continued Paul's ministry as he moved on from place to place. Even though their names may be recorded, what happened to them is largely lost to history. So let us give thanks for Sopater, Aristarchus, Secundus, Gaius, Timothy, Tychicus and Trophimus, and let us also remember all those who taught us and who took the time to help us become disciples of Jesus Christ.

Dear Lord, you long to transform our hearts and lives and turn us into living signs and citizens of your kingdom. We pray for all those who teach and preach, and we pray also that each of us may be willing and able to tell others what you mean to us. Amen.

Read 2 Timothy 4:1–8.

CR

Whoops!

A young man named Eutychus, who was sitting in the window,
began to sink off into a deep sleep while Paul talked still longer.
Overcome by sleep, he fell to the ground three floors below and
was picked up dead.

Oh dear! We probably suspected that Paul could preach for his country once he got going, but to talk for so long that his audience started falling asleep and dropping out of windows is impressive even on his terms.

However, Paul didn't seem that alarmed. He walked downstairs, held the dead boy close to him, and announced that he would be all right. Then Paul went back upstairs, shared the Lord's supper followed by a meal, and carried on where he had left off! Meanwhile, the young man revived and was taken away, no doubt by astonished and grateful relatives.

This brief vignette gives an intimate glimpse into how the early church met for worship and fellowship, albeit in somewhat unusual circumstances. Paul was setting sail the next day, and he was using every moment of the time left in Troas to teach more about the faith.

Luke reports this incident so casually that we can only conclude that it did not seem that remarkable at the time. After all, Paul had been involved with scores of miracles and healings, some of which Luke may have witnessed. Luke writes a number of passages in Acts, including the story of Eutychus, using the word 'we', which would indicate that he was actually there at the time.

If a similar incident happened today, it would certainly make the headlines, whether or not people believed it was true. Sometimes I wonder what it is that prevents more healings and miracles from taking place in our churches. Is it our expectations? Has God changed? Have we?

Dear Lord, source of all power and life, help us to expect more of you and more of ourselves when we are filled with your Spirit. Amen.

Read John 20:24–31.

CR

On the way to Jerusalem

'And now, as a captive to the Spirit, I am on my way to Jerusalem, not knowing what will happen to me there, except that the Holy Spirit testifies to me in every city that imprisonment and persecutions are waiting for me. But I do not count my life of any value to myself, if only I may finish my course and the ministry that I received from the Lord Jesus, to testify to the good news of God's grace.'

Paul was making his way eastward, as quickly as the winds and waves would take him. He was eager to be back in Jerusalem, if possible, by Pentecost. He sailed past Ephesus and landed at the nearby port of Miletus. Once there, he sent for the elders of the church at Ephesus to join him for a special meeting.

When the leaders of the churches had gathered, Paul spoke to them one last time. This is the only recorded sermon in Acts that Paul gave to Christians, and Luke himself was obviously present. In it, Paul looks ahead to difficult times for the church, and he warns those listening to be vigilant and to be aware of those who will try to entice them away from the true faith.

Paul also reminds the believers how tirelessly he taught them about the Lord, and he commends them to God's grace.

The whole tone of this address is one of a final farewell: Paul discerns that he will never return to these places and will never see these friends again. It is a sombre moment, filled with grief and foreboding.

After Paul finishes speaking, he and all those gathered kneel and pray for the last time together, and then he sets sail. Paul's overriding aim, then as ever, was to make sure that he would be able to complete the work that Jesus had called him to do.

Dear Lord, what are you calling me to do with my life—and with this day?

Read Revelation 2:1–7.

CR

Back to normal?

When our days there were ended, we left and proceeded on our journey; and all of them, with wives and children, escorted us outside the city. There we knelt down on the beach and prayed and said farewell to one another. Then we went on board the ship, and they returned home.

As Paul continues his journey, he stops off on various islands on the way to Jerusalem. When he and his friends reach Tyre, now the present-day city of Sur in Lebanon, the Christians there tell Paul not to go to Jerusalem, but he is determined. Once again, there is a farewell gathering of the whole community of believers, and once again, Paul sets sail.

For Paul, there will be no return; from now on his journeys are all one way, towards Jerusalem and finally on to Rome. But what about those who go back to their homes? What will their lives be like without Paul visiting them and writing to them? What will it be like without Paul teaching, encouraging, exhorting, inspiring and motivating them?

Sometimes I return from services or conferences filled with fresh inspiration and joy. I have a new perspective and an enlarged vision, and I know life will never be the same. But after a few days, or hours, the sparkle begins to fade and the fog of daily life begins to roll in and obscure my newly found clarity. What am I left with? For me, and all of us today, as well as for those who actually knew Paul, the test of our faith will ultimately be in the nature of our relationship with Jesus Christ. We do need other Christians, because we are part of the body of Christ, and it certainly helps to read inspiring books and go to faith-building events, but more than anything, we need to know Christ.

Dear Lord, I want to know you better. Help me to trust you enough to let you get closer to me. Amen.

Read John 14:25–27 and 17:20–26.

CR

Philip and his daughters

The next day we left and came to Caesarea; and we went into the house of Philip the evangelist, one of the seven, and stayed with him. He had four unmarried daughters who had the gift of prophecy.

We first heard about this Philip near the beginning of Acts. He had been one of those chosen with Stephen to minister in more practical ways, freeing the first apostles to concentrate on preaching, teaching and prayer. This same Philip was also the one who told a travelling eunuch about Jesus, resulting in the eunuch asking to be baptized on the spot!

Now, some time later, Philip is known simply as 'the evangelist'. It is safe to presume that he has continued in his remarkable ministry of preaching, healing and bringing people to faith in Jesus Christ. In one short factual sentence we also learn that Philip has four daughters, all of whom have the gift of prophecy. What an exciting and revealing piece of information!

A picture begins to emerge of a rather lively Christian household. Philip is one of the leaders of the church in Caesarea, and his daughters play an active role as well. We know from reading Paul's letters of the high regard in which he held prophets, and also how he expected them to behave when Christians gathered for worship. It is a clear indication that Paul expected everyone, young and old, male and female, to exercise their spiritual gifts as members of the body of Christ.

By reading through Acts, we discover that Paul ministered with and depended on both men and women, even though in some of his letters Paul writes specific instruction to churches with specific problems. This brief passage shows that it was accepted that every believer, irrespective of age or sex, can live and minister as a disciple of Christ.

Lord, please show each of us how we are to live as full, active members of your body. Amen.

Read Acts 6:5; 8:4–40 and 1 Corinthians 14:1–6, 22–33.

CR

Control issues

*We were binding sheaves in the field. Suddenly my sheaf rose
and stood upright; then your sheaves gathered around it,
and bowed down.*

Drama workshop students going through a scene are sometimes asked to decide which of the characters is in control at any one time. The one dominating stands on a chair. As the drama's plot and relationships unfold, different characters will be for ever climbing up and down. That's the stuff of drama, of life and of many Bible stories too: Joseph's ups and downs are legendary! On a more everyday level, who's in control (who's bossing who) is the subject of a million conversations—gossipy, concerned, depressed, or elated.

So, who controls us—work, friends, family, parents or in-laws? Should we let them? Whom do we control and what are the rights and wrongs of that? How do right authority and bad, manipulative control differ? What happens when we feel out of control—stress, depression, temper, apathy? How can we let God take control? We'd need six months to explore these things in any depth: we have two weeks, so let's start!

Joseph's father favoured him.

'When his brothers saw that their father loved him more than all his brothers, they hated him' (Genesis 37:4). These boys certainly didn't relish bowing down to their kid brother, even in a dream. Siblings have always vied for power—and Joseph's dad didn't exercise his control very wisely!

In the New Testament, the mother of James and John also tried to take control, asking Jesus if her sons could sit in the places of honour at his right and left hand. No, said Jesus, you've got it all wrong. My kingdom isn't about being top dog or lording it over people. It's about serving and suffering and giving your life: that's true greatness (Matthew 20:20–27).

*Lord, so much time and energy
and worry gets spent on these
control issues, not only in the
lives of people who don't know
you, but in my life too. Your way
is different—help me to understand and follow you better.*

CL

51

Being controlled—the pits!

They took him and threw him into a pit.

Once there, Joseph couldn't escape. His brothers controlled what would happen to him next—death or slavery.

Bullying has thrown far more people than Joseph into a pit. Victims of severe bullying, whether adults or children, can lose all sense of self-worth and can self-destruct, yet that didn't happen to Joseph. The next time we meet him, in his Egyptian master Potiphar's house, 'the Lord was with Joseph and he became a successful man' (Genesis 39:2). Heaven knows what Joseph must have felt when his brothers turned against him like that, but he must have held on to the fact that God believed in him and that despite appearances, God was in control, not other people.

Sibling rivalry has landed plenty of other people in deep, if less dramatic, pits. My father's older brother was so brilliant at school that Dad didn't bother trying, until war-time dangers caused a move out of London. Unaware of his genius brother, his new school found, to the family's amazement, that Dad did have a brain between his ears, after all! Last summer, a friend's difficult child became sweetness and light for one week—while her well-behaved older sister was away at Brownie camp. In my village, years ago, one grown-up sister tried to tell another what to do—and they didn't speak to each other for three decades.

Even if other people don't try to control us deliberately, our behaviour may be controlled by them. And, especially where family members are concerned, we may find ourselves in a deep pit. But, as the psalmist as well as Joseph found, there's a way out of a pit!

'I waited patiently for the Lord; he inclined to me and heard my cry. He drew me up from the desolate pit, out of the miry bog, and set my feet upon a rock, making my steps secure. He put a new song in my mouth, a song of praise to our God. Many will see and fear, and put their trust in the Lord' (Psalm 40:1–3).

CL

Control at work

Although she spoke to Joseph day after day, he would not consent to lie beside her… One day, however, when he went into the house to do his work, and while no one else was in the house, she caught hold of his garment, saying, 'Lie with me!'

Work doesn't own us, God does. Sexual harassment is only one form of wrong control sometimes found at work.

'Tell our creditors their cheques are in the post.'

'You're here to sell our product. Say it'll do anything the clients want.'

'Work comes before family.'

'Forget safety issues. Concentrate on productivity.'

Having proved himself able and trustworthy—and because God was with him—Joseph rose to a high level of authority in Potiphar's household. He was right to flee the attentions of his boss's wife, but he paid a high price. Hers was the power, so after she cried attempted rape, Joseph spent years in prison.

If we, our husbands or offspring challenge wrong aspects of the control culture at work, we may well suffer for it. A friend's daughter, having done well at university, landed a high-flying job. For her, to work until 2am and start again at 6am is nothing unusual. There's virtually no time for family, friends, church, or even boyfriend. 'How long can anyone keep going like that?' her mother worried, yet it's the culture in that line of business: changing employer would make no difference. The cost and implications of changing careers, or of refusing to keep working silly hours, is enormous—but not as enormous as submitting to wrong control out of fear, insecurity, greed or pride. In the end, God did vindicate Joseph, giving him extraordinary control at the highest level in the land.

Lord, may you rule at work. Do a control-audit in that area of our lives, helping us to dare to institute change where we are submitting to wrong forms of control—and otherwise to serve to the best of our ability, in all humility and cheerfulness.

CL

Control-change

The chief jailer committed to Joseph's care all the prisoners who were in the prison, and whatever was done there, he was the one who did it.

God was with Joseph. Whether he found himself in a palace or a prison, Joseph was marked by God as a man of authority—as he was. On the whole he coped with all the changes, the ups and downs; he trusted God and exercised his authority wisely.

What about the rest of us? Sixth-form prefects are given authority to go with their responsibilities but next year find themselves the lowest form of life at college or work. Managers face redundancy or retirement. Leaders in churches, politics or organizations finish their term of office, and often— if their sense of identity has been caught up with their role, their self-worth with their ability to control people and events— they will struggle. Women who build a dynamic career and supervise the work of others can find themselves caring for a helpless baby or elderly parent, without the benefit of line managers or underlings to relieve their 24-hour-a-day responsibility. Managers in the workplace may resent having no leadership role in their church, while those running a large church's children's work may have little say about what happens at their own children's school. From being in sole charge at home, a wife has to adapt when her submariner husband returns on leave. Parents with almost total control over their newborn child must fine-tune letting that control go, by degrees, as the years pass. I wonder if all this is God's way of teaching us to use authority wisely—not to gain our identity from it.

You might like to spend a few moments thinking about how you cope with changes in the responsibilities and areas of authority and control that you are, or have been, given. How did Joseph cope with such changes? And what does God do when his authority seems to be taken away by puny human beings? Hosea 11 seems to imply that he doesn't find these issues easy either!

CL

Right authority

So Pharaoh said to Joseph, 'Since God has shown you all this, there is no one so discerning and wise as you. You shall be over my house, and all my people shall order themselves as you command; only with regard to the throne will I be greater than you.'

Important people recognized a natural leader in Joseph—giving him authority in Potiphar's house and prison, then making him second-in-command over all of Egypt. But what exactly was it about Joseph? Why was he promoted from pit or prison to positions of power? Leaders recognized that God was with him and had marked him to be a leader, one in authority—just as the Roman army officer in Matthew 8:5–13, seeing a man both under and in authority, recognized that Jesus' authority was God-given.

Power without accountability often produces people who use control to gain more power, influence or money. But in itself authority is good, necessary and God-given, while anarchy is destructive. Anticipating desperate times of famine, Pharaoh wisely chose a godly man to take charge of the food depots. He recognized one who would act with competence and fairness. Today, when disaster hits countries where corruption and nepotism are ways of life, Christians are often called upon to distribute food, because people can see that living God's way is more important to them than selfish gain. They stand out because they view all people, not just their own tribe, friends or family, as important.

How do we handle the authority we are given, whether it's at work, with children (our own or those of other people in our care), within a church group, a club or committee, or on the governing body of a school? There may be areas where we have earned the right to speak or pray with authority. Are we, like Joseph or Jesus, relying wholly on God in doing so? Are we obeying him rather than following selfish aims of our own? How might we feel, swapping places with those under our authority?

CL

What controls us?

Realizing that their father was dead, Joseph's brothers said, 'What if Joseph still bears a grudge against us and pays us back in full for all the wrong that we did to him?'

In writing workshops, I've known mature people dissolve in tears when asked to read their work to the group. Why? Because 30–50 years previously, when they read their work to a school class, a teacher ridiculed them. Whether you're the victim or the one exercising it, wrong control can have long-term consequences.

After horribly abusing their power, it's hardly surprising that Joseph's brothers remain controlled by fear and guilt for years and years. Powerful Joseph has them quite literally at his mercy, and struggles with forgiveness, playing cat-and-mouse with them—putting silver in the sacks they take from Egypt, accusing them of theft, holding one hostage, threatening execution. Reading more of the story, we see Joseph, moved to tears, finding the grace to forgive and to want only good for his brothers. But guilt controls them still, and, with Jacob's death, they fear for their lives again.

Fear, guilt, grudges, irritation, pride, family squabbles—all of these appear as controlling influences in the story of Joseph and his family, and all can still control us today. Fortunately for Abraham's dynasty, Joseph's brothers were brave enough to ask for, and receive, forgiveness. The destructive cycle of a potential vendetta was broken as they all wept together. Joseph tells them, 'Even though you intended to do harm to me, God intended it for good, in order to preserve a numerous people... So have no fear; I myself will provide for you and your little ones' (Genesis 50:20–21). God was back in control.

Lord, I don't want to let hurts or horrible feelings of guilt or anger control me. May I let your love take control. Help me to put far away from me 'all bitterness and wrath and anger and wrangling and slander, together with all malice, and be kind to other people, tenderhearted, forgiving them, as God in Christ has forgiven me' (Ephesians 4:31–32).

CL

God in control, or us?

Then Joseph could no longer control himself.

What do you do when you feel out of control—of yourself and your own emotions, of events, or of the destructive way in which others are acting? More often than not, I mess things up, over-reacting to my own impatience or anger, my hurt or feelings of impotence. I lash out, verbally, at full volume, at whomever is unfortunate enough to be around. As a strategy, it's about as effective as using a hand grenade for a safety valve. People get hurt. So do I.

Stepping back a little in the story, what did Joseph do when floored by emotion at seeing his brothers again? He acknowledged that God was in control, and had been all along. 'It was not you who sent me here but God' (v. 8). The whole sorry tale of his being sold into slavery by his brothers, in truth, had been simply part of God's plan to rescue the whole family from a famine which only God knew was going to happen.

Whenever I feel out of control, and fail to control my own kneejerk reactions, it's because I don't trust God. If I yell at my teenagers because they are about to do something danger-ous and won't listen to me, I'd be better off praying. If I'm wait-ing for an overdue plane and there's no information, why get irate when, trusting God's tim-ing, I could settle down to a good book or conversation? When someone treats me un-fairly or misjudges me, rather than chucking metaphorical hand grenades around in self-defence, if I trusted in God for vindication I'd save all kinds of wounds, not to mention sleep-less nights. Lost or frightened, better trust in God than panic!

Father, help all of us who don't cope well with feeling out of con-trol. You are so patient with us. Help us to see you as the one in control and to release our stress to you instead of hurting our-selves and others.

CL

Controlled by the Spirit

The mind of sinful man is death, but the mind controlled by the Spirit is life and peace.

A consulting engineer friend of ours worked 87-hour weeks for nearly two months, while preparing complex reports for a multi-million-pound court case. We all worried about him, yet he appeared to be enjoying God and was eager to pray for and encourage others.

Once the report was in and the pressure off, he prayed with us for a couple who weren't yet Christians. During the course of the evening, he mentioned how his priorities have changed over the past few years. He no longer worries much about work (though it has to be done), or about promotion, status, fast cars, house or financial security. Now eternal things, like God, relationships, or enjoying the beautiful tree he sees from his office window, are more important to him—a little bit of heaven's in the office since God's there too. During that month when everyone else felt driven into the ground, although he was tired he'd lost his cool on only one occasion. We asked how he'd coped with the impossible demands that work deadlines placed upon him.

For a while now, he's started each day at the office early by praying for his colleagues. 'After all, that's where I spend most of my time,' he explained, 'and prayer changes the atmosphere. It's the way I live, rather than my words, which will reach people.' He lets God shoulder the responsibility of work, so that he doesn't worry about it 24 hours a day. He makes his priorities God's priorities and lets his mind be controlled by the Spirit. Instead of high blood pressure, he's found life and peace.

Thank you, God, that your word is true. Whether in prison cells or trapped in the agony of some chronic disease, whether struggling to feed screaming triplets or to influence boardrooms, all kinds of people who let you take control really have found life and peace. Lord, when my mind tries to wrest control back, remind me of this!

CL

Friends who control

But Martha was distracted by her many tasks; so she came to him and asked, 'Lord, do you not care that my sister has left me to do all the work by myself? Tell her then to help me.'

My daughter said of a friend who left her school some time ago, 'I've only just realized how much I used to be under her shadow.' Have you ever felt that a friend was trying to control you, in the wrong way? Some people, it seems, always want to set the agenda; to decide which clothes or food, or even people, are OK; to push their friends in a direction which, while not necessarily immoral, may be neither what those people want nor what God is asking of them.

Most of Jesus' close friends wanted to control him in some way; they 'knew what was best'! Some made desperate attempts to get him to promise them preferment in his kingdom. They urged Jesus to set up residence on the Mount of Transfiguration. They disapproved of him speaking to the woman at the Samaritan well, and tried to stop him, that last time, from going to Jerusalem. Judas wanted his own way over the group's money (and finally, much more besides). And here, in the house where Jesus came to relax among friends, one of them dared tell him to order someone else about! Martha's mind was not filled with Spirit, life and peace but with exasperation and over-busyness. Doubtless she wanted the best for Jesus, but in her own way.

How did Jesus deal with his friends' attempts to control him? He stayed filled with the Spirit, with life and peace. He stood his ground. And he affirmed those who tried to do the same. 'Mary has chosen the better part, which will not be taken away from her,' he told Martha.

Dear Jesus, help me to learn from you so that I stay controlled by the Spirit, rather than controlled by (or controlling) my friends.

CL

Control issues within marriage

Wives, be subject to your husbands as you are to the Lord.

Last week I heard on the news how police forces around England assembled all the reports of domestic violence that took place on just one day. 'A stabbing, rape or beating every twenty seconds!' the headlines screamed. And yet the real shock is that these things never normally reach the headlines: they remain hidden, year in, year out, in 'nice' and even churchgoing homes as well as deprived ones. Sometimes children are the victims but more often it's women. In nearly all cases, the perpetrators are men. Wives, be subject to your husbands? No, find help, please, now!

Of course most men never act violently. But neither (as the above text has sometimes been misused to imply) are most women as horribly manipulative as a Delilah or Jezebel. Maybe churches don't keep on about this now, but when we were first married I kept worrying about whether or not I was really obeying (being subject to) John. This got on his nerves as he tried to live out the *far* more difficult command that follows—how to love me, his wife, 'as Christ loved the church and gave himself up for her'. That wasn't preached about, and nor was verse 21: 'Be subject to *one another* out of reverence for Christ'. We observed other 'Christian' marriages where the men exercised strong control. Though not violent, they weren't godly. Obedient wives were not treated with the respect that Christ always shows towards us.

Marriage isn't about the husband dominating and the wife jumping to obey. It's about giving trust and love and wanting the best for one another, within Jesus' love and power and under *his* control. And because that's so amazingly wonderful, so intertwined with the relationship between Christ and his church and so unlike slavery, it's particularly susceptible to distortion, corruption and twisting by the evil one.

Spend time praying today for those whose marriages have gone wrong—and for protection for good marriages too. Make it a habit!

CL

Control issues—children

*His mother said to him, 'Child, why have you treated us like this?
Look, your father and I have been searching for you in great
anxiety.'*

I feel incredibly sorry for Jesus' parents here. Charged with bringing up this extraordinary child of promise, on whom so much rested, at first they had to assume complete control of his tiny form, even to the extent of fleeing abroad by night to preserve his life. Once back in their village, they settled down to more normal ways of good parenting—watching lest little Jesus hurt himself on hot cooking pots or carpentry tools, keeping an eye open as he played with other children, teaching him what was good and what could be harmful. And then, at the vulnerable age of just twelve, he went missing in the big city for four agonizing days!

Afterwards he continued to be 'obedient to them' and to increase 'in wisdom and in years'. In other words, their care and control of him didn't cease when he was twelve. He didn't stay teaching adults in his 'Father's house' in Jerusalem. But the 'missing four days' incident must have been a shocking baptism for Mary and Joseph into the painful, confusing, long-drawn-out stage of letting go.

Some parents never manage it. They still try to control grown, and even married, offspring, through emotional blackmail—'I won't be with you long'—through gifts with strings attached, or more directly. But adults must be free to make their own choices, even if those choices lead them astray—or to a cross. Without this, a real, healthy relationship between parent and offspring can't endure, and the controlling expectations of even long-dead parents can block God's plan for someone's life. 'No, my parents always told me I'm useless at that!' 'They said that unless I became a doctor or financier, I'd have failed.'

Spend some time today praying for parents who, despite anxieties, must let go. Pray for people who, having reached adulthood, remain wrongly controlled.

CL

Control issues—ageing parents

Honour your father and your mother.

Mother (in her 80s) and middle-aged daughter, in different houses. Phone rings.

Daughter: Hello, Mum. How are you?

Mother: Oh, all right, dear. Bit bruised, you know.

Daughter: Bruised? Oh Mum, you haven't fallen down again, have you?

Mother: Don't worry, just a little tumble in the garden, dear, 'cept now my arthritis is playing up something rotten.

Daughter: So what did you fall over this time? That hosepipe again?

Mother (reluctantly): Mmm.

Daughter: Look, Mum, I'll get you one of those things for winding it up. It's really easy. Will you promise me you'll use it? Only, I do worry about you tripping over in that garden of yours.

Mother: Oh no, dear, the hosepipe's twenty years old—far too stiff to wind up!

Daughter: Fine. I'll get you a new hose that's already on a reel.

Mother: Well, I don't know… 'Spose it *could* be a good idea. That old one of mine is full of holes!

Daughter: Oh, Mother, why didn't you say so before? Look, I've got to go, but I'll pop the new hosepipe in to you on Wednesday. All right? Take care now!

Mother: Bye, love!

They put the phones down. After a short pause Mother dials again.

Mother: Look dear, it's me. I've thought about it. I don't need a new hosepipe. I'll mend the holes. (*Firmly*) So don't you go buying one, all right?

This story is a true one, told me by a neighbour. So do we control or honour the decision-making of ageing parents, especially where more worrying safety issues are at stake?

Pray for carers, that they might have the wisdom to know how to act over difficult issues—and for the patience, support and strength they need, too.

CL

Lead by serving, not controlling

'You know that the Gentiles lord it over them, and their great ones are tyrants over them. It will not be so among you; but whoever wishes to be great among you must be your servant.'

She didn't discover Jesus until well into middle age. When the pastor of a small church introduced her to the Saviour, she was over the moon. But a couple of years later she wrote to me, a virtual stranger, distraught. The same pastor was wanting to control every aspect of her life and work—her thoughts, even. Spiritual power is strong and can be used for good or evil, to build up or to manipulate or destroy. The woman didn't want to abandon faith in Jesus but recognized that the pastor's oppressive control was attacking her very self. She's happily following Jesus in another church now, but if she hadn't cried for help she might well have gone under.

Wrong control exercised by church leaders can be a frightening thing. Jesus' life, by contrast, was a stark demonstration of how leaders in God's kingdom should differ from those in the harsh Roman Empire. 'The Son of Man came not to be served but to serve, and to give his life as a ransom for many,' our passage continues. Shortly before his crucifixion, Jesus washed his disciples' feet—a job not undertaken by most servants, only the lowest of the low. How astonishing that Jesus would wash away the grime of the day from the feet of friends he knew would betray or desert him. Why would the Lord of all do that? He told them why: to set an example. Most of them would lead, eventually, but it had to be in an attitude of serving others, not lording it over them.

Lord, help us to foster that same serving attitude that you displayed so astonishingly. Footwashing isn't in our culture as it was in yours. Show us, as we wait on you now, practical ways in which we can serve others.

CL

Who's in control?

'He trusts in God; let God deliver him now, if he wants to; for he said, "I am God's Son."'

During Holy Week, when some of the Bible passages about the events leading up to Jesus' death are read, listen out for who is in control at any one time. Is it Judas or the Pharisees? Pilate or Herod? The Sanhedrin, the mob or the Roman soldiers? First one, then another gains the upper hand. One thing's for sure, God, his angels and Jesus all seem powerless.

And yet, looked at from the point of view of Easter Day, who's in control? What incredible strength Jesus must have had to keep silent like a sheep before shearers. He let himself be tried unjustly, mocked, whipped, stripped, raised high for all to see in his agony—and then abused by the very people he was trying to help. He could have called for an army of angels to blast our whole galaxy to kingdom come—never mind the Roman army or the puny religious authorities. As for his Father, what love for humanity could have informed his strength of resolve to hold back and let all this happen, until his Son declared it finished—or 'accomplished'? Jesus bowed his head and *gave* up his spirit (John 19:30). No one can control or kill God!

The same strength, the power that raised Jesus from the dead, is at work in us, even when we feel powerless and utterly out of control, even when others belittle and shame us. It empowered radiant Stephen as he was stoned to death. It empowered Peter, who lost control of his own courage and then became a pillar of the church.

Thank you, Lord, that your great power doesn't lord it over us. You never impose your will; you serve and lay down your life. We're so grateful that it's you who are ultimately in control, for you are good, full of mercy and lovingkindness. May we yield more and more to your control.

CL

Not bread alone

The tempter came and said to him, 'If you are the Son of God, command these stones to become loaves of bread.' But he answered, 'It is written, "One does not live by bread alone, but by every word that comes from the mouth of God."'

Our readings over the next two weeks are scattered through the Gospels, describing varied events in Jesus' life: celebration, miracle, teaching, situations both ordinary and extraordinary. They have one thing in common—food!

Most of us notice if a meal is delayed or a tea-break missed. But Jesus was in the hot, arid desert for a month without food. The words here are strong: 'He was famished.' We do not know how Jesus really felt. Was he so aware of his hunger that it was a great struggle for him when the devil—in whatever guise he came—suggested that Jesus might use his divine power to satisfy his own need? There were plenty of stones lying around; just one would have made a meal. It reminds me of our two-year-old son eyeing some freshly baked biscuits: 'Just look. Just count. Just one, just two, just three, just eighteen.' Isn't that the insidious way in which temptation often comes? Jesus knew that 'just one' would

be misuse of his power. Or was he so focused on seeking his Father's will that the temptation was merely a trifling distraction?

Either way, he was clear on the source of his strength. 'One does not live by bread alone, but by every word that comes from the mouth of God.' These were no mere words to him. He demonstrated his statement by his readiness to quote scripture and in his goal to live in tune with his Father. 'My food is to do the will of him who sent me and to complete his work' (John 4:34). His Father's will was everything to him; his Father's word was not merely his guideline but his sustenance.

Please help me, Lord Jesus, to follow you and to be nourished by God's word.

                                    RG

Food for a crowd

Taking the five loaves and the two fish, he looked up to heaven, and blessed and broke the loaves, and gave them to the disciples, and the disciples gave them to the crowds.

It is easy, when we read a passage as familiar as this, to assume that we know all about it. Before you go any further, read the whole story again. What does it tell you about Jesus?

- His need to be alone with God (v. 13).
- His willingness to be interrupted (v. 14).
- His compassion: a wonderful word that means 'deeply moved in the guts' (v. 14).
- His power to heal (v. 14).
- His challenge to his disciples, to stretch their faith: 'You give them something' (v. 16).
- His trust in God: as soon as he knew the extent of the meagre provisions, he told the people to be seated; he prayed—and then started the distribution, sure that there would be enough for the whole crowd (v. 19).

Someone counted carefully. How many people were there? Maybe ten thousand! ('About five thousand men, besides women and children.')

How amazed the disciples must have been as they saw the food multiplied! Even the remaining debris, twelve basketfuls of crusts and fishbones, was more than they had to start the meal.

Look again at Jesus. Which of his characteristics do you share? Do you long to spend time alone with God in the middle of your busy life? How flexible and patient are you when you are interrupted? Do you risk being moved in your guts by the need of strangers? Do you expect to see God at work in healing (of bodies, emotions and relationships)? Do you have the courage to confront and to challenge other people, or do you prefer to play it safe and allow them to stay in their comfort zone? Do you trust God enough to step out in faith when you do not know the outcome? Do you trust him to provide for your needs?

Thank you, God, for your Spirit, who can enable me to become more like you.

RG

A lesson in trust

When the wine gave out, the mother of Jesus said to him,
'They have no wine.' … His mother said to the servants,
'Do whatever he tells you.'

The wedding feast was in full swing. The food was plentiful, but disaster struck. The wine caterer's calculations were wrong and supplies ran out. What an embarrassment for the host! His reputation for hospitality would be marred. As she watched the scene, Jesus' mother saw the worried servants anxiously pouring the last drops from the wine jars. So, trusting her son to have an answer, she told him what was happening. He gave her a surprisingly brusque reply: 'Woman, what concern is that to you and to me?' But she was not to be deterred. She continued to trust him, and told the servants to do what he told them. She was sure he would act.

That was enough. He gave orders to fill with water the six enormous jars, then to draw some off and take it to the butler. The butler tasted it, and found it to be even better wine than they had drunk at the start of the banquet. That was not the normal way to do things. Serve the best wine first, when the guests' palates were sensi-tive. Then, as the alcohol began to deaden their senses, they would be less discerning and the cheaper wine could safely be served.

Trust from Mary. Trust, too, from the servants. As they began to draw off the liquid, they could see that it looked different. But they could not be sure of its quality. After all, good wine takes many months to mature. This was immediate. How would the butler react? Would they be in danger of losing their jobs if it tasted like vinegar? But they obeyed, a mark of their trust.

Finally, 'his disciples believed in him' as they saw Jesus' stature and power displayed in the first of the 'signs' recorded by John.

To think over: On what basis is your faith in Jesus grounded? How does it lead you to act?
RG

Healed to serve

Simon's mother-in-law was in bed with a fever, and they told him about her at once. He came and took her by the hand and lifted her up. Then the fever left her, and she began to serve them.

There had been a dramatic scene in the synagogue. Jesus was teaching with an authority to which the congregation was not accustomed, when he was confronted by shouts from a man who was under the control of an evil spirit. But the confrontation was short-lived and the man was freed. Here was another level of the demonstration of Jesus' authority.

Afterwards Jesus went to the home of Simon and Andrew's extended family. He might have hoped for a rest after the pressures of the morning. But at once they told him that Simon's mother-in-law was ill. Maybe they were apologizing for the lack of ready refreshments. Jesus immediately went to her, held her hand, lifted her up—and she was well. She did not sit around expecting other people to look after her. 'She began to serve them': a basin of water and a towel to wash their dusty feet, cold drinks, a meal. And Jesus was refreshed and helped to prepare for the intensive evening ahead.

I like the attitude of unselfish service in this story. We see it in Jesus, who came straight from challenging ministry in the synagogue and went on to even more demanding ministry after sunset, when the sabbath was over. We see it in the woman, who went straight from her bed to the kitchen. They did not demand any rights of rest or special treatment. They responded without complaint to the need they saw. Do we follow their example?

Teach us, dear Lord, to follow your example and always to be ready to serve others.

RG

Live to eat?

*He took her by the hand and called out, 'Child, get up!' Her spirit
returned, and she got up at once. Then he directed them to give
her something to eat. Her parents were astounded; but he ordered
them to tell no one what had happened.*

Jairus, as a leader in the synagogue, was a respectable churchman. In our day he would have been a churchwarden or an elder. He had heard the authority of Jesus' teaching; he had seen miracles of healing. Now he needed Jesus, desperately. His only child was dying. It must have been hard for him to wait while Jesus, who had already started towards his house, stopped to help a shy, unimportant woman; even harder when one of his servants arrived to tell him that his daughter was dead. How far could he trust Jesus' encouraging words? 'Do not fear. Only believe, and she will be saved.' Healing he had seen; renewed life, from death, was outside his experience.

At Jairus' house, Jesus passed the noisy crowd of hired mourners. Only the parents and his three closest disciples were allowed into the girl's room. They watched with amazement as he spoke to her, lifted her up, saw her revive. At this point Jesus had a number of concerns.

She was weak after her illness: she needed food. The parents were feeling helpless: they needed a practical task. The mocking mourners were not ready to hear of a dead person coming alive again: better for them to think that a coma had been wrongly diagnosed as death. Jesus was not ready for a dramatic, possibly distorted story to be spread round.

'Give her something to eat' is only a small detail in this story of faith and divine power. But it reminds me that our Saviour is not only the divine 'up-there' God who looks down on us with all-seeing eyes. He has shared human life, and he knows what it is like to live with our difficulties and our encouragements.

---

*Lord, thank you that you know
our exact needs.*

RG

Whatever it costs

'You gave me no kiss, but from the time I came in she has not stopped kissing my feet. You did not anoint my head with oil, but she has anointed my feet with ointment. Therefore, I tell you, her sins, which were many, have been forgiven; hence she has shown great love. But the one to whom little is forgiven, loves little.'

Jesus, a dinner guest of Simon, a Pharisee, was reclining in the normal fashion of the day—head towards the table, feet facing out. Amazingly, Simon had omitted the common courtesy of providing water and a towel for guests who arrived in open sandals from dusty roads. The ex-prostitute ('a sinner') didn't have water; she had tears of joy and gratitude. No towel, but her long hair. She probably had little money, but she expressed her devotion to Jesus by lavishing expensive perfume on him.

Jesus' tale of two debtors made the point very clear. Simon's deficient hosting was the result of his inadequate awareness that Jesus had anything to offer him. He thought he was all right as he was. The woman knew her life was a mess, that Jesus could forgive and change her. The story faces us with clear questions. How deep is our own allegiance to Christ? On what is it founded? How do we show it?

As always, I am struck by Jesus' poise. Most of us would be highly embarrassed to be singled out for such a public display of emotion. He was totally at ease, in a way that speaks of his own inner confidence and peace.

What can I give him,
poor as I am?
If I were a shepherd,
I would bring a lamb.
If I were a wise man,
I would do my part.
Yet what can I give him—
give my heart.
CHRISTINA ROSSETTI

RG

Today is the Women's World Day of Prayer. The theme this year is 'Challenged to Reconcile' and has been prepared by the women of Romania. The Bible readings are 1 Samuel 25:1–35; 2 Corinthians 5:18–20; and Ezekiel 36:25–28.

Tell your friends

Then Levi gave a great banquet for him in his house; and there was a large crowd of tax collectors and others sitting at the table with them. The Pharisees and their scribes were complaining to his disciples, saying, 'Why do you eat and drink with tax collectors and sinners?'

One day, Levi, known to us better as Matthew, was sitting at his booth, collecting the taxes on behalf of the Roman overlords—and, incidentally, making himself rich on the side. This was the common practice among the tax collectors of the day; hardly surprising that they were disliked. It is not clear whether Jesus' magnetism and authority were enough for Levi to decide to follow him at a first meeting, or whether he had already been watching from a distance. But Luke tells us that 'he got up, left everything, and followed him'. That is pretty decisive!

Levi's cheating had given him a big house; maybe parties were his speciality! So he invited his friends—the ones who were on the outside of respectable society —to meet his new master. We do not need to be old established Christians to invite in those we would like to become Christians too. In fact, it is often the longstanding Christians who have

few 'not-yet-Christians' among their friends. The good news about Jesus can become stale news to them, while Jesus' new followers share Levi's excitement and desire to share Jesus with others. I think of a hard-drinking, hard-swearing young woman who in her first year as a student was ready to sleep with anyone. She discovered Jesus, and her life was so changed that she became one of the most effective evangelists in our church, as her lips and her life together spoke about Jesus. She knew from her own experience that Jesus had come to 'call not the righteous, but sinners to repentance'.

Lord, please help me to become more effective in demonstrating you in my life and in speaking about you to those who do not follow you.

RG

An evil deed

Herod feared John, knowing that he was a righteous and holy man, and he protected him… The king was deeply grieved, yet out of regard for his oaths and for the guests, he did not want to refuse her.

Another dinner party—of a very different character! On his birthday the king gave a banquet in his palace in Tiberias, on the shores of Lake Galilee. I guess that Herod and his important guests were well dined and well wined when Salome, who was both his niece and his stepdaughter, came to entertain them with her seductive dance. They so applauded that Herod —maybe to show his appreciation to her, maybe to vaunt his generosity before his guests— made a magnanimous offer. 'I swear I'll give you anything you want, up to half my kingdom!'

Phew! What an amazing offer, Salome thought. Apparently incapable of making her own choice, the young woman went to her mother. 'What shall I ask for?' This was just the opportunity to exterminate John that Herodias had wanted! She had been furious at his bold rebuke over the marriage. 'You could have a very unusual gift. Ask your stepfather for John's head!' Salome was clearly on her mother's side and under her influence. She wasted no time with her demand.

Herod was aghast. It was one thing to imprison John, quite another to execute him. But Herod's reputation got the better of his integrity. What would his guests think if he broke his oath? How would his wife and stepdaughter treat him? So his orders went out, and John was immediately beheaded.

We can reflect on two things: the relationships within the family, and the motives of individuals. Are any of these strands reflected in your own family or your own life?

Lord, please help me to bring change through the power of your Spirit.

P.S. If you want to know how Herod's life ended, read Acts 12:19–23. Food again—for the maggots.

RG

Rules in perspective

Jesus went through the grainfields on the sabbath; his disciples were hungry, and they began to pluck heads of grain and to eat. When the Pharisees saw it, they said to him, 'Look, your disciples are doing what is not lawful to do on the sabbath.'

The Old Testament commandment was clear. The sabbath was to be a day set apart for God; a day for rest, not work. The principle is clear, but its application in our lives is more blurred. The Pharisees were rigid in their interpretation, as of many other aspects of God's laws. For example, journeys of more than three quarters of a mile were among the multitude of prohibitions for the sabbath.

On this occasion, Jesus and his disciples were walking through the grainfields—watched suspiciously by the Pharisees. Feeling peckish, the men picked some ears of corn and began to nibble. 'Ah! Reaping and threshing! Against sabbath rules!' complained the Pharisees. Like many legalists since, they were so anxious to study what scripture said that they could not hear what it meant. The disciples were not breaking God's law, merely the Pharisees' regulations.

Jesus brought to their attention two Old Testament situations. David, evading Saul, went to the tabernacle and lied about his situation in his request for food. The only bread available was the shewbread, set aside for the priests, which the high priest gave him. The second reference is to the fact that on the sabbath the offerings were doubled. Extra work for the priests that day! Human need on the one hand, the worship of God on the other, both took precedence over regulations.

What does all this have to say to our own Sunday 'sabbath'? In my early days as a Christian my rules for Sunday verged on the legalistic. Nowadays I am far more flexible. I wonder whether I am living more in line with God's principles or whether I have merely succumbed to the pressures of our 21st-century secular society. What about you?

Lord, please show me how you want me to keep Sunday special.
RG

Joy and jealousy

'Now his elder son was in the field; and when he came and approached the house, he heard music and dancing. He called one of the slaves and asked what was going on. He replied, "Your brother has come, and your father has killed the fatted calf, because he has got him back safe and sound." Then he became angry and refused to go in.'

Each of the two men in this familiar parable is typical of his place in the family. The older son was hard-working, obedient, conformist. The younger one was free-spirited and irresponsible. You probably know the story well. The younger son took his share of the expected inheritance, treating his father as if he were already dead. Years later, with his money wasted and a famine in the country, he was on his beam-ends. He trudged home in sorrow, asking his father for nothing better than life as a servant.

The welcome he received astounded him! His father was overjoyed. Fine clothes, new sandals, and the best delicacies for a feast: nothing was too good for the restoration of this lost son. His older brother was even more astonished. He had worked unceasingly, but he had never been honoured like this! He was too angry even to listen to his father's pleading.

The father's love, forgiveness and generosity, pictures of our heavenly Father, are the main thrust in this story. There are warnings, too. The dutiful older son had played his part well. But was there underground resentment lurking? 'It's not fair! My brother goes off to enjoy himself and I just slave away here!' Resentment is like a destructive cancer. I know. My own resentment was a deep drain on my spirituality, when my husband was free to go away on exciting 'God trips' while I stayed at home with young children. Like the older brother, I came to the point when my resentment exploded in anger. Mercifully, God changed me.

'Forgive each other; just as the Lord has forgiven you, so you also must forgive' (Colossians 3:13).

RG

Who gets in?

'"The wedding is ready, but those invited were not worthy. Go therefore into the main streets, and invite everyone you find to the wedding banquet." … But when the king came in to see the guests, he noticed a man who was not wearing a wedding robe, and he said to him, "Friend, how did you get in here without a wedding robe?" And he was speechless.'

Jesus told this three-part story during a series of confrontations with the Jewish religious leaders. They were furious with him, but afraid.

Stage 1: The king invited his well-off friends to a wedding banquet. But when the feast was ready, they all made excuses: 'My business… My new wife… I have more important things on hand.' The king tried again but his servants were murdered. The enraged ruler sent his army to kill the 'select' guests.

Stage 2: 'Go and invite anyone you find, even the unemployed and the gossip-makers out on the streets.' They came—all sorts. Whatever they were wearing, shabby or smart, they were offered the official wedding garments to cover their own clothes.

Stage 3: The king went to meet his new guests. One man there had spurned the king's clothes; he clearly thought his own were grand enough. The king was as angry with him as he was with those originally invited, and his end was as decisive.

The wedding banquet is a picture of the kingdom of heaven. Who will enjoy the celebrations? Not the 'select' religious, self-righteous ones who manage their lives by their own rules and priorities. The invitation is open to everyone. But all enter on the same footing. Our right to enjoy the heavenly celebration is dependent on God the king's gracious, undeserved invitation and on our willingness to accept the 'robe of righteousness' that he offers us through Christ. Our own 'clothes' of good deeds, however worthy, can never be good enough for the holy king.

Nothing in my hand I bring,
Simply to your cross I cling.
Naked, come to you for dress,
Helpless, look to you for grace.
A.M. TOPLADY (1740–78)

RG

A meal for all time

He took a loaf of bread, and when he had given thanks, he broke it and gave it to them, saying, 'This is my body, which is given for you. Do this in remembrance of me.' And he did the same with the cup after supper.

The build-up to this Passover meal was intense. The disciples had all been among the huge crowds in the temple courts, where Jesus had taught, boldly, prophetically. They were surely aware of the ever-increasing hostility of the Jewish leaders. They had probably noticed Judas' occasional absences and wondered where he had gone. They knew of the mysterious provision of the upstairs room for their meal together.

Together they ate the meal—roast lamb, bitter herbs, unleavened bread. Then Jesus made a startling statement. 'I have eagerly desired to eat this Passover meal with you before I suffer… I will not eat it until it is fulfilled in the kingdom of God' (vv. 15–16). 'Before I suffer… fulfilled in the kingdom of God'. What was he saying? They were puzzled, and they waited for the familiar ceremony to continue. 'This is the bread of affliction…'.

But they did not hear the expected words. Instead, 'This is my body, which is given for you.

Do this in remembrance of me.' No longer was this meal to be the memorial of the Israelites' deliverance from four hundred years of slavery in Egypt. It was to be instead the memorial of the Christians' deliverance from slavery to sin. The Passover lamb was killed annually. Christ the Lamb of God was 'offered once to bear the sins of many' (Hebrews 9:28). During the ritual of the Passover meal, several cups were drunk, each with its own significance. Now there was to be one cup, 'the new covenant in my blood', said Jesus.

This story is so familiar that the words can almost bypass us. So close your eyes and imagine the scene. Then move straightaway to picture the cross. Thank him afresh for this meal. Thank him afresh for his death.

RG

Their eyes were opened

When he was at the table with them, he took bread, blessed and broke it, and gave it to them. Then their eyes were opened, and they recognized him; and he vanished from their sight. They said to each other, 'Were not our hearts burning within us while he was talking to us on the road, while he was opening the scriptures to us?'

It had been a perplexing, roller-coaster week for the disciples. Jesus' triumphal entry into Jerusalem. Growing tension in the temple courtyard by day. Peaceful evenings in Bethany. The Passover meal together. The grief of Jesus' arrest and crucifixion. Now there was astounding news that the tomb was empty, even that Jesus had been seen alive. What was going on?

Cleopas and his companion (maybe his wife Mary) had plenty to talk about as they started on their seven-mile walk home. Suddenly a stranger caught up with them. They were amazed that he seemed to know nothing about Jesus, the talk of the town. They told him about the disappearance of Jesus' body, the appearance of the angels and about their own confusion.

Then the stranger started to talk. Not noticing the distance or the time, they listened spellbound as he spoke from one bit of scripture after another about the Messiah, showing them how Old Testament history and prophecy were being fulfilled. When they reached their village they wanted to hear more: they invited him in. They sat down to eat. Then the man who had so enthralled them 'took bread, blessed and broke it'. In that act, they recognized him. It was Jesus; he was indeed alive. The angels had spoken truth.

He vanished. Forgetting their tiredness and hunger, ignoring the dark, they immediately set off to retrace their steps to Jerusalem. Excitedly they shared the news with their friends, only to hear that Peter, too, had seen him.

Jesus' resurrection is a fact of history that I never questioned. But I still remember my excitement when I recognized that Jesus was alive to be my friend. Does that ring bells with you?

RG

Do ghosts eat?

'Touch me and see; for a ghost does not have flesh and bones as you see that I have.' … While in their joy they were disbelieving and still wondering, he said to them, 'Have you anything here to eat?' They gave him a piece of broiled fish, and he took it and ate in their presence.

The disciples were reeling from the tale their two friends had brought of their meeting with Jesus on their journey. They were both frightened and excited. The door was locked against the Jewish leaders (John 20:19). Suddenly another figure appeared. It looked like Jesus. Was it his ghost?

Jesus knew just what they were thinking. 'Don't be afraid. See me. Touch me. I'm no ghost.' Then, to emphasize his reality, he asked for food; they watched while he ate the fish. Then he went on to teach them, and they began to understand afresh truths from the scriptures.

This story gives us a glimpse to help answer Paul's question in 1 Corinthians 15:35, as he writes of resurrection for Christians: 'How are the dead raised? With what kind of body do they come?' Jesus had certainly died, although he was buried quickly, before rigor mortis set in. Now he was alive—but in what sort of body was his spirit clothed? He was recognizable (though not always immediately), by voice as well as by sight. He could be touched. He could eat. There was something 'really human' about him. But at the same time this 'spiritual' body could pass though locked doors; he could appear suddenly ('from nowhere' we might say) and vanish just as suddenly ('into thin air'). To put these 'real' and 'spiritual' bodies together is outside our human comprehension. It is like the relationship between the seed that is planted and the plant that grows—recognizable, but transformed; 'sown perishable, raised imperishable' (1 Corinthians 15:42).

Lord, I don't fully understand all this. But thank you for the amazing transformation you make in me—now in my character, and in my body after I die.

RG

Acts 9:36–43 (NIV)

The mother hen ministry

In Joppa there was a disciple named… Dorcas, who was always doing good and helping the poor. About that time she became sick and died… All the widows stood around… crying and showing (Peter) the… clothing that Dorcas had made while she was still with them.

At this time of year we are encouraged to thank our mums and give them flowers, but Mothering Sunday can be painful for people whose mothers let them down. My mum was multi-gifted and I adored her sparkling personality, but during my growing years she was either busy or absent. Throughout her last twenty years, illness made her so dependent on me that she called *me* Mummy! But I did not lack mothering—because of Marjorie. A friend of my parents, she 'adopted' me when I was 17, and for forty years she was everything a mum could be. When my six children were growing up, she was always there ready to listen to my moans and pray for the baby who wouldn't sleep, the toddler with asthma or the obnoxious teenager. She never gave advice; she just listened, loved and spoilt me with little treats and kindnesses. Last week I lost her and, like many others who grieve, this Mother's Day is going to be tough.

Dorcas obviously gathered many fragile chicks under her comforting wings, and her mother hen ministry is needed in every church—but most of us can't manage more than one chick! What you can't get you can always give, and many people who mourn, or always lacked, a mother figure often become such a figure for others. As a young and often frazzled mum, I desperately needed the steady support of an older woman, but actually age is irrelevant when providing this kind of spiritual and practical cherishing. Older people who have outlived their loved ones can be seriously short of affection, and to be 'adopted' and cherished by a younger friend can be deeply healing.

Could God be asking you to become a mother hen to someone else? Why not ask him?

JRL

His mother's name was...

(Azariah) was sixteen years old when he became king, and he reigned in Jerusalem fifty-two years. His mother's name was Jecoliah... He did what was right in the eyes of the Lord... Manasseh was twelve years old when he became king, and he reigned in Jerusalem fifty-five years. His mother's name was Hephzibah. He did evil in the eyes of the Lord.

The Old Testament usually finishes describing the adventures of the kings by telling us two things: whether they pleased the Lord or did evil in his sight; and their mother's name. By linking these two pieces of information, is the Bible telling us that mothers like Jecoliah and Hephzibah had a massive influence on their sons' spiritual destinies? Manasseh had a very godly father but he certainly didn't take after him!

Yet there is a danger that mothers can feel smothered by this responsibility. Of course children with Christian mothers have many advantages, the most important being prayer. My grandmother began to pray for her eight children the moment she suspected they were conceived. 'Paying into their spiritual bank account,' she called it —and her children and grandchildren are still benefiting. We also take our children to church activities, read Christian books and live out our faith in practical ways but we have to remember that God gave human beings the gift of choice. Many mothers do all the 'right things' but *still* their children turn away from God—and we usually blame ourselves! If only we realized that, while we are responsible for modelling God's love to our children, we are *not* responsible for their choices.

Lord I hold out to you the children you have given me to love and I ask that, throughout life, they may do what is right in your eyes. Help me to make you real to them. I can't always be there to care, guide and protect them, but you can. So I hold them up to you on open hands, not in tight, controlling fists. Amen.

JRL

Branded by his mother

His mother called his name Jabez, saying, 'Because I bore him in pain.' And Jabez called on the God of Israel saying, 'Oh, that you would bless me indeed, and enlarge my territory, that your hand would be with me, and that you would keep me from evil, that I may not cause pain!' So God granted him what he requested.

We don't know this mother's name but we do know that she had such a frightful labour that she called her son 'Pain-giver'. Poor child! Every time anyone asked why he had such an odd name, he'd have to say, 'Because I gave my mum so much pain.' The feeling that he was destined to cause trouble and misery to those he loved obviously bothered him. Many of us grow up 'branded' by the attitudes and remarks of parents and teachers. They may not actually christen us 'Unwanted', 'Should-have-been-a-boy', 'Thick', or 'Not-good-enough', but the way they feel about us influences the way we see ourselves in later life.

That panics me! Did I permanently damage my children? Probably; but Jabez gives us all hope. God can heal the emotional scars we leave on others. No one has to be stuck with a bad self-image because of their childhood: like Jabez, we can ask God to change us.

For the last three months I've been praying Jabez's prayer every day. When my husband left me, I felt 'branded' as a failure. After a major grief it is easy to shrivel up inside and withdraw from other people to protect ourselves from further pain. So, like Jabez, I've been asking God to enlarge me (expand my love towards others) and to protect the relationships I still have. I want to catch this man's huge desire for God and the faith that God can undo the damage that others do to us—or that we have done to them.

Why not stick the 'Jabez prayer' on your fridge door to remind you to ask God every day to heal your scars and expand your life?
JRL

Control

*Herodias nursed a grudge against John and wanted to kill him...
Finally the opportune time came... Herod gave a banquet... When
the daughter of Herodias came in and danced, she pleased Herod...
He promised her with an oath, 'Whatever you ask I will give
you...' She went out and said to her mother, 'What shall I ask for?'
'The head of John the Baptist,' she answered... (The executioner)
went, beheaded John in the prison, and brought back his head on a
platter. He presented it to the girl, and she gave it to her mother.*

Ouch! The Bible contains some awful mothers but Herodias beats the lot! This was her daughter's big moment: she should have asked for something that would have benefited her future life. Instead, her controlling mother used her to fulfil her own goal—revenge. But when we point an accusing finger at someone, three of our fingers point back at us!

Do we ever try to live out our lives through other people? We've all heard of the mothers who never became ballerinas, tennis stars or musicians but who force their children to do it for them. A surprising number of adults feel bound by other people's expectations or feel failures because they fail to live up to them. Recently I met a nursing sister who efficiently runs a ward in a London hospital but suffers from bouts of depression because she feels she let her mother down. 'She wanted me to be a doctor,' she explained, 'but I never made the grades.' Another friend, whose husband died when her children were teenagers, told me that ten years on, she realized she was still using them as emotional props. 'I had to made a definite decision to let them go; then to fill the void with God himself.'

It is not only mothers who use and control other people; 'mother hens' can too. I've seen women 'take on' a new Christian or a young mum and instead of carrying out a normal discipling role they have totally dominated the other person's life in order to meet their own desire for control.

Think about your various relationships and ask yourself, 'Who controls me and whom do I control?

JRL

Nightmare!

Abraham… sent (Hagar) off with the boy. She went on her way and wandered in the desert of Beersheba. When the water in the skin was gone… she thought, 'I cannot watch the boy die.' And as she sat there nearby, she began to sob… God opened her eyes and she saw a well of water.

Have you ever been stuck in a ghastly situation that you can't control or understand, and you can't find a way out? Every time you solve one problem, you create ten more, while the 'why' questions buzz in your head like wasps! When the nightmare concerns a child you love, the sense of powerlessness is overwhelming, and often the worst part is the feeling that God just doesn't care. Hagar must have felt all this as she sobbed in despair (v. 16). Theologians have always argued about why she was alone out there in the wilderness, and who was to blame— Abraham, Sarah, Ishmael, Hagar herself or God. Whoever it was, Hagar must have felt terribly hurt and rejected. The sense of 'this isn't fair' often adds to the pain of these situations, and our resentment can cut us off from God's comfort.

The first time Hagar had been lost in this desert was when she ran away from her mistress (Genesis 16), but God met her and told her what to do. Amazed that he knew her name and cared so intimately for a mere runaway slave-girl, she had called the place 'The God who sees me'. I've heard preachers say, 'Why did she forget about God's care?' but in these agonizing situations we don't always think straight. When my fourth baby was seriously ill, I felt I didn't have enough faith to pray, but 2 Timothy 2:13 helped: 'If we are faithless, he will remain faithful'. I realized that it is not our faith that counts but God's faithfulness! He could still see Hagar, even though she had temporarily lost sight of him—and he showed her the solution (v. 19).

The next time you feel trapped in one of these nightmares, stop struggling with the 'whys' and the 'hows'. Try asking God into the middle of the mess and leave him to sort it out in his own time.

JRL

God the mother

Can a mother forget the baby at her breast and have no compassion on the child she has borne? Though she may forget, I will not forget you! ... As a mother comforts her child, so will I comfort you; and you will be comforted.

My fourth baby screamed incessantly. The only way I coped was by carrying him all day on my back, papoose style, where he invariably slept 'resting between my shoulders' (Deuteronomy 33:12).

The debate about whether God is male or female always irritates me because he can be everything we need him to be at different stages of our lives. He uses familiar human relationships to model the infinite variety of his love: he tells us he wants to be our Father, friend, husband, lover, brother, boss and king. Today's verses show that he can also mother us. Sometimes, when we have lost our mothers, or were never adequately mothered by them, we have an empty, lost feeling inside, and I am convinced that God can fill the emptiness with the gentle, tender side of his love. But we have to choose to let him.

Over the last few years I've lost several of the most important people in my life. While I want to allow God to fill the gaps they have left, sometimes I think, 'He isn't enough! I can't see, feel or hear him!' It is easy, then, to search for new human relationships to fill the vacuum, often with disastrous consequences. So I quickly pray, 'Lord you promised to comfort those who mourn, so I *choose* to run to you for that comfort.' Then I find that he either floods me with peace or sends someone to cherish me on his behalf.

Lord, I want to be like a baby kangaroo, hidden in your pocket.

Now read Psalm 131.

JRL

A mother to Jesus

*'For whoever does the will of my Father in heaven is my brother
and sister and mother.'*

When I think of the high value psychologists and theologians put on the role of a mother in a human's development, I often wonder what was so very special about Mary that she should be chosen, above all other women, to care for Jesus. He stayed at home with her until he was thirty, so the bond between them must have been very close indeed. She even stood at the foot of the cross, in case he needed her, in spite of the agony that it must have caused her.

Today's passage is hard to understand unless we realize that the brothers of Jesus did not, at first, believe he was God. When he became massively popular, they said, 'He's out of his mind' and set off, with Mary, to 'take him away' (Mark 3:21). They could not get to Jesus because of the crowds and he did not go out to them because he knew exactly why they had come! Instead he said something that many of us find strange. We are all happy to be his servant, friend, sister or child, but we are mystified when he calls us his mother. How can we 'mother' Jesus?

Even though my three sons have left home, they still seem to need me. When they lose a girlfriend, lose a job or face some big decision, home they come to offload on Mum, because they know that I'll listen and *mind* for them. But do we 'mind' about the grief Jesus faces every day? Prayer, on one level, is asking him to do things for us or others; a deep layer of prayer simply keeps him company, as a mother might sit with her son. Going even further, we can actually share the pain he feels as he looks at a suffering world and then weep with him.

Could Jesus come to you to be mothered sometimes, and sit with you, allowing you to share his load of grief and comfort him with your love?

JRL

John 11:17–19 (NIV)

The body of Christ

Many Jews had come to Martha and Mary to comfort them in the loss of their brother.

Jerusalem was not far from Bethany. To visit Martha and Mary at the time of their bereavement was a natural thing to do for first-century Jews—part of their culture. It is not so natural for us now. We live in an individualistic society. Grief, loss, hardship of any kind are considered personal things. Besides, it is easier not to get involved. What would we say? What if we said the wrong thing?

Maybe we can learn something from the example of those first-century Jews. Jesus calls us to love our neighbour—and that includes the friend who has just lost her child or whose husband has walked out on her. But what can we say? Religious platitudes often do more harm than good. Sensitivity is called for and the willingness to be God's ears and hands as well as God's mouth. Just being there, showing that we care, can make a world of difference. We can show our care by offering practical help, taking the children to school, doing a pile of ironing... Being God's hands can take many forms.

After my father had died, many of my friends knocked on my door just to give me a hug. Then they went again. It was all I could cope with. Others came and said, 'We don't know what to say, but we share your pain because we love you.' What more did they need to say? Others helped in practical ways. A number of my friends prayed for me every day. A bookmark with the following text, given to me at that time, has meant a lot to me: the people who just sat and wept with me, holding my hand, they were the people who helped.

We are the body of Christ. By one Spirit, we were all baptized into one body. Let us then pursue all that makes for peace and builds up our common life.
ALTERNATIVE SERVICE BOOK 1980

KP

If only…

'But I know that even now God will give you whatever you ask.'

If only he had left home a bit earlier, then he wouldn't have had that terrible accident. Or, even worse, if only I had not kept him, he would have left a bit earlier. These kinds of reproaches are often heard from those who are bereaved. They cannot believe that their friend or relative is really dead, so they come up with reasons why it should not have happened. It's a natural but not a helpful reaction.

Martha does not stop at accusing Jesus. In the second sentence, there is a glimmer of hope, maybe even a hidden request: 'Not all is lost, for God will give you whatever you ask. Go on, ask!' Martha is desperate, yes, but also full of faith. She knows that her 'if onlys' will not bring Lazarus back to life. Only Jesus can do the impossible and work a miracle. Martha is sure of that.

What do we do when faced with loss? Do we complain, feel sorry for ourselves, try to wish it away? Or do we turn to the one who can work a miracle?

Martha had asked her question. Now she had to wait. How would Jesus react? Would he say, 'I will raise Lazarus from the dead, right now'? Or would he say, 'Sorry, can't help you here'? In fact, he says neither of those things, but that is not the point. Martha could do nothing more but trust God for the outcome. She can't have found that easy. It would have been easier to revert to more 'if onlys'. Asking God and then trusting him involves risk, and is one of the biggest challenges of the Christian life. But it is worth taking on this challenge. Go on, ask!

'And we know that in all things God works for the good of those who love him, who have been called according to his purpose' (Romans 8:28).

KP

I believe

'I am the resurrection and the life. He who believes in me will live, even though he dies.'

What a statement! It was not unusual for Jews to believe in the resurrection. It was an item of dispute for some—the Pharisees believed in the resurrection, the Sadducees did not. Martha will have been familiar with traditional Jewish belief on this subject. In fact, her instant response to Jesus' initial question (v. 24) reflects this belief. But Jesus' statement goes much further. He does not comfort Martha by pointing at the resurrection in some distant, unobtainable future. He says instead, 'I am the resurrection—and I am standing in front of you.' Resurrection and life here and now, through Jesus, and in the face of death, with Lazarus lying in the tomb, dead and buried. Traditional Jews would have been shocked by Jesus' claim. Not so Martha. She answers by affirming her belief and acknowledging that Jesus is the Christ: 'Yes, Lord, I believe you are the Christ.'

We might be almost too familiar with the message of the gospel. Let us not forget how radical it was in Jesus' day and still is in our day. Be honest—are you not afraid of death? It is not something we like to think about. We might simply be afraid of what might happen tomorrow, never mind death. Whatever may happen tomorrow, however long we might live on this earth, one thing is certain: Jesus is the resurrection and the life. We will live, even though we die. He offers us life in abundance (John 10:10). We can have real life, now, through him.

Jesus has not promised us an easy, pain-free life. He makes no promises to Martha at this stage. She questions him no further but goes back inside the house to call Mary. Martha has shown her extraordinary faith and her recognition of who Jesus is—the Christ, Messiah, Saviour of the world.

Take time today to place all your worries into Jesus' hands and thank him for giving you life in abundance.

KP

Being real

Jesus wept.

He wept. In public. And he was a man. How embarrassing. Simon, a vicar, well respected, admired by many, one who seemed to 'have it all together', had to interrupt his sermon. It was one of the first sermons he had preached since the death of his mother. He paused and wept. His congregation respected him even more after this sermon. Simon had shared a part of himself that otherwise often remained hidden. He was grieving, suffering, hurting. He was real.

As women, we are often better at showing our emotions than those men who were told, 'Boys don't cry' when they were little. Yet even for us it can be difficult to be open about what goes on inside. For years, I did not want to admit how I really felt, not even to myself. Too painful, too dangerous. I might lose control. Well, when I did lose control, and tears came, what a relief it was. Those who knew respected me more, not less. They had seen the real Kristina and they liked her better than the pretend one they had seen before. There is nothing wrong with emotions.

Why do we think we have to pretend we can cope with everything all the time? Who are we trying to fool? Of course, there are times in life when we just have to grit our teeth and get on with the task at hand. Work needs to be done, children need to be cared for, dinners need to be cooked, even when we feel like hiding in a corner and crying. But these times of pulling ourselves together need to be balanced with times of letting go. Jesus was not afraid to be real. Try it! You will be surprised.

We can only be real if we are not afraid of other people's reactions. Pray that God will give you the inner security that comes from knowing that you are his beloved daughter.

KP

But…

But some of them said, 'Could not he who opened the eyes of the blind man have kept this man from dying?'

But why…? But how…? Why not…? Could you not…? How could she…? Jesus must have been exasperated by those questions—many of them asked in order to trap him. Whatever their motives, there were always people who knew exactly what he should have done. Even as he was hanging on the cross, there were those who sneered at him and explained what they would have expected him to do (Luke 23:37; Mark 15:29).

'If your Jesus is such a wonderful God, why didn't he intervene in the war in Kosovo?' 'Why is there such poverty in Africa when God loves everybody?' Or, closer to home, 'Why didn't he heal little Johnny of his cancer?' You might have heard questions like these from your non-Christian colleagues, friends or members of your family. These could be genuine concerns but more often than not, people just use them as 'proof' that God cannot be who we know he is—our loving Father and the maker of the universe, omnipotent and omnipresent. It is hard to know how to respond and requires a lot of sensitivity as we often don't know what is behind the questions. Do they serve as excuses not to deal with the message of the gospel, or do they cover up other, deeper questions? It is often worth probing to find out why the original question was asked.

Being a Christian is not always easy. We will meet people who reject the good news of Jesus and who will sneer at us and reject us because we are followers of Christ. We should not be surprised at that. We are called not to respond with the same rejection but to show Jesus' love by our words and our lives.

'The ways of the Lord are right; the righteous walk in them, but the rebellious stumble in them' (Hosea 14:9).

KP

The glory of God

Then Jesus said, 'Did I not tell you that if you believed,
you would see the glory of God?'

Martha has just affirmed her belief that Jesus is indeed the Christ. Now, a few minutes later, she seems to have lost all faith. When Jesus stands in front of the tomb and asks for the stone to be rolled away, she does not expect a miracle. Quite the opposite: 'By this time there will be a bad odour, for he has been there four days.' What has happened to her faith? Was it not genuine?

Her faith was genuine enough. However, she found it hard to see beyond the obvious, to go below the surface of the meaning of Jesus' words. She had difficulties connecting her faith in the Christ to everyday life. Yes, Jesus was the Son of God. But would that change anything right now?

Jesus is the resurrected Christ, now, in 2002. Does that make a difference to our lives? Can we see beyond the obvious and get a glimpse of the 'bigger picture'? Martha did not realize that Lazarus had to die to reveal the glory of God. We often don't understand what has happened, don't understand how God could have *let* this happen, don't understand how our daily worries, big and small, might fit into God's plan. May I suggest that sometimes, more often then we think, events happen in order to reveal the glory of God?

Martha did not (yet) know the outcome. If she had, she would not have worried about the smell from the body of Lazarus. We often cannot know the outcome of events. What we can know, however, is that Jesus' life, death, and resurrection make a difference to our lives. And we can be part of events that reveal the glory of God. What a privilege!

For yours, Lord, is the power, the glory and the majesty, for ever and ever. Amen.

                                    KP

New life

'Lazarus, come out!'

God definitely has a sense of humour. Can you imagine Lazarus coming out of the tomb, probably more hopping than walking, possibly bumping into things because the grave clothes tied his legs together and obscured his vision? This is a comical and at the same time awesome scene. Lazarus had experienced the depth of death and had come back to life again.

How must he have felt, stumbling out of the tomb? Overwhelmed? Confused? Maybe even reluctant to come out? I think there is one thing we can be certain about: life after this experience would never be the same again. Lazarus had been given new life, a second chance here on earth. But let him speak for himself:

'I heard his voice calling me. It was not a loud voice, but, how can I say it… it sounded urgent, compelling. I knew I had to obey it. There was no doubt about that. I wasn't quite sure where I was, it was all dark. I got up and found that I could hardly move! My legs were bound together and so I moved forward with some difficulty. Half shuffling, half hopping, I moved towards the voice calling me. It became lighter around me but I still could not see. There were other people there, not just him. I stood there, trying to listen to what the voices where saying, trying to make sense of it all. Finally, after what seemed like a long time to me, a hand gently started to take away what had bound me. I could see, I could move, I could walk again. I saw people around me and they were weeping. I saw plants, trees, the sky—it was all so beautiful. And I saw Jesus, looking at me, just looking at me.'

Could this not be a description of somebody coming to Christ? What can we do to take away what binds others? What binds us?

What would Martha have felt at this point? Reflect.

KP

The triumphal entry

The next day, the news that Jesus was on the way to Jerusalem swept through the city, and a huge crowd of Passover visitors took palm branches and went down the road to meet him, shouting, 'The Saviour! God bless the King of Israel! Hail to God's ambassador!' Jesus rode along on a young donkey, fulfilling the prophecy… His disciples didn't realize at the time that this was a fulfilment of prophecy; but after Jesus returned to his glory in heaven, then they noticed how many prophecies of Scripture had come true before their eyes.

Jesus began his last week on earth by riding into Jerusalem on a donkey. He chose a time and a place where many people could see him; and crowds went out to meet him, because they had heard about the raising of Lazarus from the dead (vv. 17–18). The people cheered and waved palm branches to welcome a king who they thought would free them from the tyranny of the Romans.

It must have been an amazing experience to be a participant in that crowd, caught up in the excitement of it all. But the ordinary people had misunderstood who Jesus was and why he had come. The disciples were only marginally clearer after Jesus tried to explain his impending death to them (John 12:20–50).

Later, after Jesus rose again, the disciples had time to sit and put events into a larger context. They realized that their scriptures had clearly pointed to the fact that Jesus was the Messiah; he had fulfilled many prophecies in very precise ways.

Jesus' words and actions took on new meaning and made sense for the disciples. Think about the events in your life. How has God led you to this point? Are there things he promised you that have happened without you noticing? As we grow older and look back on our lives, we see God's involvement much more clearly than in the press of current events.

Spend some time thanking God for his faithfulness, that he leads us and fulfils his promises.

AS

Jesus washes the disciples' feet

Jesus said, 'And since I, the Lord and Teacher, have washed your feet, you ought to wash each other's feet. I have given you an example to follow: do as I have done to you. How true it is that a servant is not greater than his master. Nor is the messenger more important than the one who sends him. You know these things— now do them! That is the path of blessing.'

The night of Passover, Jesus knew that it was his last night on earth. He was gathered with his disciples for the Passover meal. Jesus had loved his disciples from the time he had called them (v. 3), and he continued to love them completely and utterly, right to the end, even though he knew that Judas was about to betray him.

To show the special way in which he loved his disciples, after the meal, Jesus rose, took off his outer garment and washed the disciples' feet as if he were a servant. But he knew his disciples would not fully understand his actions until after his death and resurrection.

Firstly, Jesus wanted to demonstrate to them the 'once and for all' cleansing that the unique shedding of his blood would achieve for those who believed in him (1 Peter 3:18). In dying on the cross, Jesus humbled himself utterly (Philippians 2:7–8) and showed that he loved

the world by laying down his life for undeserving humanity (John 15:12–13).

Secondly, Jesus wanted to give his disciples a practical picture of his example of humility and what this implied for believers. If Jesus was willing to humble himself and take on a task that most people would recoil from, how much more should his followers learn to love others enough to do the same? Because Jesus has saved us by his sacrifice, we are to show our gratitude by serving others.

Give me a pure mind—that I may see you; a humble mind— that I might hear you; a loving mind—that I might serve you; a faithful mind—that I might be found in you.

DAG HAMMARSKJÖLD

AS

Jesus promises the Holy Spirit

Jesus said, 'If you love me, obey me; and I will ask the Father and he will give you another Comforter, and he will never leave you. He is the Holy Spirit, the Spirit who leads into all truth... You (recognize him), for he lives with you now and some day shall be in you. No, I will not abandon you or leave you as orphans in the storm—I will come to you.'

Jesus had been preparing the disciples for his death: he had fulfilled prophecy in the public view, given teaching on the Kingdom and practical demonstrations of love and humility. He had indicated that he knew what lay ahead, but was ready to do the Father's will. He reassured his disciples that although he was leaving them, they would not be abandoned; he would send them the gift of the Holy Spirit.

Only by receiving the Holy Spirit would the disciples have the ability to remember, understand and put into action all the things that Jesus had taught them (v. 26). The Holy Spirit is not just the one who reveals Jesus to the believer, but the one who strengthens the believer in times of difficulty, gives guidance and peace when situations are difficult and perplexing, and most of all, offers comfort when we feel alone.

I love Psalm 139:7–10: 'I can never be lost to your Spirit... if I ride the morning winds to the farthest oceans you are there.' These verses were of great comfort when I had to travel halfway round the world to go 'home' from boarding school to the Western Pacific where my father worked. I managed it because I had the promise that God's Holy Spirit would go with me in the plane and stay with me the whole time I was on that distant atoll. Whatever our situation, God's Holy Spirit is always with us.

Thank you, Lord, that you never fail us or forsake us. Thank you that your Holy Spirit is there, especially when life is difficult, speaking peace to our hearts. Amen.

AS

Jesus prays

Jesus said, 'I have given them [the disciples] your commands. And the world hates them because they don't fit in with it, just as I don't. I am not asking you to take them out of the world, but keep them safe from Satan's power… make them pure and holy through teaching them your words of truth. As you sent me into the world, I am sending them into the world, and I consecrate myself to meet their needs for growth in truth and holiness.'

Jesus has given the disciples, and us, his commands. He reminds us of what he has taught us when we read his word and listen to the prompting of the Spirit he has given us. When we live according to Jesus' commands, we find that we do not fit in with the world any more. Our hearts and minds have been changed by the cleansing power of Jesus' forgiveness. As such, we become living accusations against the world's morality, even without speaking a word.

Jesus knows that it will not be easy for us to live a 'different' life in a fallen world, but he does not ask the Father to take us out of that difficult situation. What Jesus does pray is that we will be protected from Satan's power as we live for Jesus.

We are sent into the world to be salt and light (Matthew 5:13–16), but Jesus has not sent us out to face our difficulties alone. He has consecrated himself: that means he has set himself apart to meet our need for growth in truth and holiness. Growth in truth and holiness is not an option. We grow most when we are facing difficulties, but only if we are depending on and listening to the words of truth that make us pure and holy.

Thank you, Lord, that you have committed yourself to our growth in truth and holiness. Help us to work with you as you work to change us from one degree of glory to the next. Amen.

AS

Peter denies Jesus

So the Jewish police, with the soldiers and their lieutenant, arrested Jesus and tied him... they took him to Annas, the father-in-law of Caiaphas... Simon Peter followed along behind... and stood outside the gate. The girl watching at the gate... let Peter in. The girl asked Peter, 'Aren't you one of his disciples?' 'No,' he said, 'I am not!' ... By the fire he was asked again... 'Of course not,' he replied. But one of the household slaves... asked, 'Didn't I see you in the olive grove with Jesus?' Again Peter denied it. And immediately a rooster crowed.

Despite all the encouraging words that Jesus had spoken to the disciples, they were not to realize the full power of what they had been told until after the resurrection. Now, when Jesus was arrested, all but two fled. Peter and the 'beloved disciple' followed Jesus to Caiaphas' house. We do not know what happened to the 'beloved disciple', but when challenged by the household servants, Peter denied Jesus three times.

Peter had sworn he was ready to die for Jesus (John 13:37), and he was ready to do just that in the Garden of Gethsemane when he drew a sword and cut off someone's ear (John 18:10). It seems that Peter had completely misunderstood what Jesus had meant when he talked about his death. Peter was ready to rise to a violent encounter, but after Jesus' reprimand (John 18:11),

Peter's probable confusion led him to be unprepared for the quiet, unexpected challenge in the courtyard that caused him to deny that he even knew Jesus.

I once did something similar. I was with a group of teenage friends who didn't know Jesus. One girl asked, 'No one around here's one of those Jesus freaks, are they?' 'No!' I said, loudly, not wanting to be excluded from my peer group in that community. As it was, I was so ashamed of myself, I withdrew from the group anyway.

Lord, you know what we are going to say before we even say it. Give us courage by your Holy Spirit, to answer as we should. Amen.

AS

The crucifixion

They crucified him and two others with him, one either side with Jesus between them… Standing near the cross were Jesus' mother, Mary, his aunt, the wife of Cleopas, and Mary Magdalene. When Jesus saw his mother standing there beside me, his close friend, he said to her, 'He is your son.' And to me he said, 'She is your mother!' And from then on I took her into my home.

One of the only things that all four accounts of the crucifixion have in common is that there were women standing near the cross. In all the Gospels except John, the women are 'standing at a distance', but in John's Gospel, the women are close enough to hear the quiet words of Jesus as he hung there.

Even in his dying agony, Jesus had concern for others. In Luke 23:39–43, Jesus shows compassion for one of the thieves who died with him. In today's passage we see Jesus showing concern and compassion for John and for his own mother, Mary. Jesus told Mary to care for John as if he were her son, and he told John to care for Mary as if she was his mother. The relationship would involve love, respect and responsibility.

John took Mary into his own home. It might not have been easy for Mary to give up her own home, or for John to adjust his circumstances, or for the other members of John's household to adapt to the new situation; but they did so because Jesus asked them to.

Our families are precious gifts from God. Nothing we are involved in is so important that we can excuse ourselves from giving our families proper care and attention. If the suffering Christ could make time for such matters, so should we. Are we standing close enough to him to hear clearly the quiet instructions he may have for us concerning our wider family and friends?

Lord, set your cross in the midst of our families, that in dying to self, we might learn to serve and love you better.

AS

The burial of Jesus

Afterwards Joseph of Arimathea, who had been a secret disciple of Jesus for fear of the Jewish leaders, boldly asked Pilate for permission to take Jesus' body down; and Pilate told him to go ahead. So he came and took it away. Nicodemus, the man who had come to Jesus at night, came too, bringing a hundred pounds of embalming ointment made from myrrh and aloes. Together they wrapped Jesus' body in a long linen cloth saturated with the spices, as is the Jewish custom of burial.

Here are two men radically changed by Jesus' death, rather than just his life. Joseph of Arimathea was a member of the Jewish Council who had not agreed with their accusations against Jesus. He was actively seeking the Kingdom of God (Luke 23:51). Nicodemus, a Pharisee, went with Joseph to bury Jesus' body. He was the man who had come to see Jesus by night (John 3:1–21) and been told that 'God so loved the world, that he gave his only begotten Son, that whosoever believeth in him should not perish, but have everlasting life' (AV).

We will never know exactly what these two men witnessed in Jesus' death that changed their clandestine faith to one that was willing to face Pilate to ask for the body of Jesus. It is possible that the Holy Spirit finally opened their hearts to understand the things Jesus had said. Maybe, like the centurion, seeing Jesus' final moments, in which he redeemed the world, was enough to convince them that Jesus was truly the Son of God.

Many people look to Jesus' life as a model to live by, but it is only when we face Jesus' death that our lives are really changed. When we dare to look at the cross, we cannot help but acknowledge our need of salvation and acknowledge the wonderful way the Father has provided to bring us back to him.

Lord, when we consider your cross, we cannot hide any longer. Bring us out of the darkness in which we conceal ourselves, into your wonderful light.

AS

Christ is risen, alleluia!

We ran to the tomb to see; I outran Peter and got there first, and stooped and looked in and saw the linen cloth lying there, but I didn't go in. Then Simon Peter arrived and went on inside. He also noticed the cloth lying there, while the swath that had covered Jesus' head was rolled up in a bundle and was lying at the side. Then I went in too, and saw and believed [that he had risen]—for until then we hadn't realized that the Scriptures said he would come to life again!

When Mary Magdalene came to the tomb, she found the stone rolled back. She ran to tell the disciples that someone had stolen Jesus' body. John's Gospel does not say whether Mary looked inside and saw that the body was missing, or whether she only saw the removed stone and assumed the rest.

Peter and John wanted to see for themselves. John was more hesitant, perhaps worried about the implications of what he might find. Peter went straight in to check things out. He noticed that the cloths were lying in a way that could only mean that the body had not been unwrapped by another person.

Eventually, John went in too. Seeing the grave cloths laid out as they were led him to believe that Jesus must have risen rather than being taken. Then they began to remember what

Jesus had told them and what the scriptures pointed to—a risen Messiah.

Our response to the resurrection can be like any of these three people's. We might take a brief look and jump to the wrong conclusions. We might be keen to know what happened, but hesitate at the thought of the implications. Or we might be desperate to let the evidence give a verdict, but remain completely baffled at the direction in which it leads us. It is only when we let the word of God and Jesus himself direct us that we will be able to believe.

Holy Spirit, lead us into all truth. Help us to understand the full wonder of Jesus' risen life. Amen.

AS

Why are you crying?

*Mary had returned to the tomb and was standing outside crying.
And as she wept, she stooped and looked in and saw two white
robed angels sitting at the head and the foot of the place where
Jesus' body had been lying. 'Why are you crying?' the angels
asked her. 'Because they have taken away my Lord…' she replied.
She glanced over her shoulder and saw someone standing behind
her. It was Jesus, but she didn't recognize him. 'Why are you
crying?' he asked her. Whom are you looking for?' … 'Mary!'
Jesus said… 'Master!' she exclaimed.*

Mary returned to the tomb after Peter and John had left. She obviously hadn't met them on the way, because she was still upset that someone had taken Jesus' body. She looked into the tomb to check that her eyes hadn't deceived her, or perhaps to see if the body had been returned. The two men Mary saw sitting there were surprised to see her crying. Jesus had risen and they seemed to expect her to know.

Then Mary sensed someone behind her, who was also surprised to see her crying. She didn't recognize Jesus until he spoke her name. Perhaps Jesus looked different, or perhaps Mary didn't recognize him because she didn't expect to see him.

Often we need to revisit the place of our grief, actually or emtionally, to be sure of the circumstances. If we are brave enough to take a closer look, we may find that things are not quite the way we first assumed. Jesus himself meets us in those gloomy surroundings. We may fail to recognize him because we are not expecting to see him there, but if we listen hard enough we will hear him speak our name: we are not alone. Hope and a glimmer of understanding begin to replace confusion and despair. Knowing that the risen Lord is with us enables us to walk out of the tomb into the sunshine to bring a message of joy to others.

Lord, did you give me this unfathomable loneliness in order that I might be able to give you everything with greater ease?

DAG HAMMARSKJÖLD

AS

Jesus appears to the disciples

That evening the disciples were meeting behind locked doors, in fear of the Jewish leaders, when suddenly Jesus was standing there among them! After greeting them, he showed them his hands and side. And how wonderful was their joy as they saw their Lord! He spoke to them again and said, 'As the Father has sent me, even so I am sending you.' Then he breathed on them and told them, 'Receive the Holy Spirit.'

Despite the testimonies of Peter and John, and Mary's account of seeing the Lord, the disciples were gathered behind locked doors because they were afraid of the Jewish leaders. Perhaps Peter, John and Mary had imagined it all: grief can do strange things to the mind. Perhaps the Jewish leaders would round them up and demand that they produce Jesus' body—something they didn't possess. What had really happened? What did it all mean, and what would become of them all?

Suddenly Jesus stood among them. The door was locked: how had he got in? Was it really him? Jesus greeted them in a way that was familiar and precious to them. He showed them his wounds—things that could not be counterfeited so as to fool those who had stood by and watched him die. It was the Lord!

Jesus told them that he was sending them as his Father had sent him—no more hiding behind doors locked from the inside, no more fear of the authorities. To give them the strength to spread the good news of the forgiveness of sins, and to endure the suffering, Jesus breathed his Holy Spirit upon them.

What are the things we are frightened of and hiding from? Do we feel confused about the present, uncertain about the future or concerned that we might be blamed for something that we are have no hand in?

Risen Jesus, stand with us in our locked hearts. Breathe your Spirit over us, and help us forgive those we hold to blame. Help us to walk out in your strength to fulfil what the Father has planned for us.

AS

Believe!

One of the disciples, Thomas, 'The Twin', was not there at the time with the others. When they kept telling him, 'We have seen the Lord,' he replied, 'I won't believe it unless I see the nail wounds in his hands—and put my fingers into them—and place my hand into his side.' ... The doors were locked; and suddenly, as before, Jesus was standing among them and greeting them. Then he said to Thomas, 'Put your finger into my hands. Put your hand into my side. Don't be faithless any longer. Believe! ... Blessed are those who haven't seen me and believe anyway.'

Maybe you feel like Thomas—everyone else has wonderful, faith-building experiences, but somehow you manage to get left out. This passage was included in the Gospels just for you! Jesus doesn't want anyone to miss out on all that he has won for us, and just as he knew Thomas' struggle to believe what he was being told, Jesus knows and understands the things we struggle with that stop us coming to fullness of faith.

I expect Thomas was quite belligerent. He made his statements about wanting to touch Jesus' wounds as a way of emphasizing how unlikely he found their story, and how much convincing he was going to need to believe it. When Jesus appeared to the disciples again, when Thomas was present and the door locked, and quoted back to Thomas the conditions he had previously stipulated, I expect Thomas didn't need to touch Jesus to believe. He could only fall on his face and proclaim Jesus as Lord and God.

We can often be as belligerent as Thomas and make ridiculous statements challenging Jesus to prove that he is who he claims to be. It is not that we can't believe; it is more that our rebellious, perverse nature doesn't want us to believe what, deep down inside, we know to be true.

Lord, prevent us being awkward for awkwardness' sake. Make us like little children, with hearts ready to believe the 'unbelievable'. Amen.

AS

Breakfast with Jesus

*At dawn we saw a man standing on the beach but couldn't see
who he was. He called, 'Any fish, boys?' 'No,' we replied. Then
he said, 'Throw out your net on the right-hand side of the boat,
and you'll get plenty of them!' When we got (to the beach), we
saw that a fire was kindled and fish were frying over it, and there
was bread... 'Now come and have some breakfast!' Jesus said.
Then Jesus went around serving us the bread and the fish.*

Perhaps Peter was tired of sitting behind a locked door and wasn't quite sure what Jesus had meant when he said he was sending them out into the world, or how that was to happen. So he and the others decided to go back to the thing that most of them knew how to do well... fishing.

At dawn they encountered Jesus. He told them to cast the net out on the other side of the boat. When they did, it was full to bursting. John remembered that this had happened when Jesus had called him, his brother James and Simon Peter to follow him (Luke 5:4–7). Back on the beach, Jesus shared out bread and fish, which reminded them of the time he had fed the five thousand. The fact that he himself served them was consistent with what they knew of his nature (John 13:14). They were sure it was Jesus, but dared not ask.

Perhaps you are in a situation where you have met Jesus and started to follow him, but the way he is pointing you is unclear or slow in coming. We might feel that the only option is to go back to what we used to be or used to do. But our experiences with Jesus have changed us and led us on. In these times of waiting, Jesus calls to us, reminds and reassures us with familiar words and deeds that he has a definite plan for our future.

Lord, in your way and in your time, that's how it's going to be in my life. Amen.

AS

Jesus and Peter

Jesus said, 'Simon, son of John, do you love me more than these others?' 'Yes,' said Peter, 'you know I am your friend.' … Jesus repeated the question: 'Simon, son of John, do you really love me?' 'Yes, Lord,' Peter said, 'you know I am your friend.' … Once more he asked him, 'Simon, son of John, are you even my friend?' … Peter was grieved at the way Jesus asked the question this third time. 'Lord, you know my heart; you know I am,' he said.

Although Peter was overjoyed to see Jesus, he must have had a nagging ache in his heart, knowing that he had previously denied he knew Jesus. Jesus never allows this sort of business to remain unresolved. Jesus asks Peter three times whether he really loves him—one time of asking for every denial.

The first two times Jesus questions Peter, he uses a word for 'sacrificial love'. Knowing he has failed Jesus, Peter can only reply with the word that indicates that he loves Jesus as a brother. The third time Jesus questions Peter, Jesus uses the same word as Peter and implies, 'Are you sure you love me only like a brother, despite what you have done? I know you love me more than that!' Peter is now almost despairing, and tells Jesus that he knows that Jesus can tell what is hidden in his deepest heart—a real love for Jesus that was being strangled by a sense of failure.

Although we don't read about Peter asking Jesus directly for forgiveness, we can sense that there is deep reconciliation going on here. In drawing out Peter's real feelings, Jesus is able to convey to Peter that he is forgiven and that he should also forgive himself. Only then will Peter be free to move in the power of the Holy Spirit to fulfil the commission that Jesus has given him.

Lord, you know our hearts, you know who we really are. Draw out of us and forgive us those things that hinder us from fulfilling your plan for our life.

AS

A future with Jesus

[Jesus said] 'When you were young, you were able to do as you liked and go wherever you wanted to; but when you are old, you will stretch out your hands and others will direct you and take you where you do not want to go.' Jesus said this to let him know what kind of death he would die to glorify God. Then Jesus told him, 'Follow me.' Peter asked Jesus, 'What about him, Lord?' … Jesus replied, 'What is that to you? You follow me.'

Jesus spoke these words to Peter to indicate to him what would happen to him in the future—that he would end his life by glorifying God, not failing him. We know from the history books that this is true. The Romans martyred him on a cross. Peter insisted that he be crucified upside down, because he did not feel worthy of dying the way Jesus did. Peter did follow Jesus, and the remainder of his life, as well as his death, glorified God.

Like Peter, however, we can at times be over-concerned with what the Lord has planned for other people's lives. Will they be called to greater service, greater faith, greater prominence, greater blessing than we are? Jesus tells us not to compare our calling with that he has given to others.

Our own calling is specifically tailored for the person that God the Father made us. No one else can do what the Lord has planned for us to do, however small, insignificant or peculiar that calling may seem to us or to others. Only when we reach heaven will we perhaps be given the privilege of seeing what our obedience in the small and menial things—as well as the big, impressive things—achieved in the spiritual realm. Whatever Jesus has called you to do, *you* follow him, and never mind about what he is asking everyone else to do!

Lord, constrained or free, help me to keep my eyes on you and the tasks you have called me to. Amen.

AS

Confidence and freedom

Although I am less than the least of all God's people, this grace was given me: to preach to the Gentiles the unsearchable riches of Christ... In him and through faith in him we may approach God with freedom and confidence.

In the film *The Shawshank Redemption*, there is a poignant episode when Brooks is released from prison after spending fifty years inside. After decades of having his every move dictated to him, he suddenly has freedom to make his own decisions. But after only a few weeks of liberty he climbs on to a chair and hangs himself. Before he dies he writes to his old friends in prison: 'I'm so tired of always feeling afraid.' Life outside was too strange for him. He was used to the world of prison and felt at home there. He couldn't make the adjustments necessary to live as a free man. He was utterly friendless and always looking over his shoulder in fear, wondering what new and strange experiences each day would bring.

Here is an example of someone who has freedom but no confidence to embrace what that freedom offers.

How many of us believers are like Brooks? We know we have been delivered from sin by Christ's sacrifice, and we are therefore free from condemnation and judgment. Colossians 1:13–14 tells us, 'For he has rescued us from the dominion of darkness and brought us into the kingdom of the Son he loves, in whom we have redemption, the forgiveness of sins.' We are out of the prison, but how confident are we to approach our holy God and stand before his great white throne? Our sins have been forgiven, but how many of us live with needless guilt? How many of us fear what God might ask us to do if we gave ourselves unreservedly to him and put him in the driving seat of every area of our lives—job, marriage, time, holidays, future, money?

Is there something that is robbing you of confidence in God's presence? Bring this fear to him and ask for his forgiveness.

CP

Confident yet humble

To some who were confident of their own righteousness and looked down on everybody else, Jesus told this parable: '… I tell you that this man, rather than the other, went home justified before God. For everyone who exalts himself will be humbled, and he who humbles himself will be exalted.'

There is nothing worse than a smug Christian—someone who smiles beatifically, saying, 'I'm going to heaven. God loves me.'

Jesus reserved his sternest comments for the Pharisees who were so proud of their scrupulous obedience to God's law that they'd forgotten they were sinners in need of forgiveness. They thought that obeying God made them better than other people. They became proud and complacent and looked down on others.

Christians can often be accused of being hypocrites. We affirm that we believe in a God of love and mercy, yet our lives often demonstrate the opposite. We are critical or judgmental about anyone who doesn't fit our chosen mould of Christianity, let alone those who have not yet embraced the gospel. Our confidence before God needs to be firmly anchored in Christ's death and resurrection, not our obedience or good deeds.

When I was a missionary in Africa I was sometimes, figuratively, put on a pedestal by other Christians. They thought a missionary must be a few steps nearer to God than ordinary mortals. It is easy to start believing that God is extra pleased with me because I've made significant sacrifices for him. This is complete and utter rubbish.

When we talk about being confident that God loves and accepts us, we need to express it with a humble, grateful attitude. It needs to be abundantly clear to everyone that we are not confident in our own righteousness but in his mercy and grace to a hopeless sinner.

Not the labours of my hands
Can fulfil thy law's demands;
Could my zeal no respite know,
Could my tears forever flow,
All for sin could not atone;
Thou must save, and Thou alone.
Nothing in my hand I bring;
Simply to thy cross I cling.
A.M. TOPLADY (1740–78)

CP

108

Inspire confidence

'Be strong and courageous. Do not be afraid or discouraged because of the king of Assyria and the vast army with him, for there is a greater power with us than with him. With him is only the arm of flesh, but with us is the Lord our God to help us and to fight our battles.' And the people gained confidence from what Hezekiah the king of Judah said.

Words can hurt, words can heal. In the changing-room at half-time in a football cup final, one can imagine the words the coach uses to inspire and encourage the team. If you are two goals down, you can feel tired and defeated before you even start the second half. But the right word from the coach galvanizes the team. They burst out on the attack and score a goal. Tiredness is forgotten as motivation surges through the team and they go from strength to strength.

Hezekiah chose inspiring words when the Israelites were facing a huge army. Humanly speaking, they were doomed. No doubt they were terrified and had perhaps given up and were preparing for surrender. You can't fight well if you are discouraged and already defeated in your mind.

They needed a pep talk from the king. But encouragement had to be based on fact, not on wishful thinking. Hezekiah hit the right note: God was far stronger than the enemy, and he was with them.

How about our words? At work, at home or with friends, do our words encourage or discourage? Are your encouragements based on good evidence? Do we turn people to God when they are in difficulty? How are you using this great gift of speech that God has given you? 'Watch the way you talk, let nothing foul or dirty come out of your mouth. Say only what helps, each word a gift' (Ephesians 4:29, *The Message*).

Lord, I pray that today you would give me words to help people gain confidence in their particular situation and that each word I utter would be a helpful gift.

CP

Confidently facing fear

The Lord is my light and my salvation—whom shall I fear? The Lord is the stronghold of my life—of whom shall I be afraid? … Though an army besiege me, my heart will not fear; though war break out against me, even then will I be confident.

What scares you? Cancer, financial problems, teenagers going off the rails, getting old? Probably few of us can relate to King David's situation. He feared invading armies and war, suffering the humiliation of defeat and being robbed of his possessions, deported, even killed.

We know that he did suffer defeat at the hands of his own son! That is a mighty humiliation. In the same way, some of the things we fear may happen to us. How could David be confident and not afraid? How can we walk confidently into an unknown and potentially difficult future?

David was not saying, 'The Lord is my light and my salvation, my stronghold, therefore my life will be stress-free with no problems and nothing bad will ever happen to me.' He seems to be saying, 'When war comes, my ultimate confidence is in God, and his good plans for me; therefore I will not fear because he is with me as my stronghold in whatever situation I face.'

A Christian friend announced to me that she was giving up her faith. When I asked 'Why?' she said, 'Because God didn't give me what I wanted.' In her case, what she wanted was a godly husband. How many of us are like my friend? We want God to make life nice and cosy for us. To judge from some of the adverts on telly, one would assume that life should be great fun and we should always have what we want, because we're worth it. Life is not like that for anyone, but with God as our stronghold we can face whatever comes with confidence, just as David did.

Lord Jesus, I bring to you my fears of ……………… Thank you that you are my light, my salvation and my stronghold, so I am safe with you.

CP

Confidence in God = fruitfulness

Cursed is the one who trusts in man... He will be like a bush in the wastelands... But blessed is the man who trusts in the Lord, whose confidence is in him. He will be like a tree planted by the water that sends out its roots by the stream.

There is a stark contrast here between the one who puts confidence in human endeavours and the one who trusts God. One life will be barren and dried up, whereas the other will be always fruitful and life-giving.

Living in Wales, I don't often get the opportunity to see what happens to plants when they get insufficient water: we have abundant rain! But even here it is obvious that the banks of rivers are very fertile places—the trees are strong and green even in times of relative drought.

The analogy here is that just as the tree pushes its roots nearer and nearer the source of water, so we should strive to put our spiritual roots deep into God. The tree draws up nourishment from the stream and that produces leaves, blossom and fruit. As we tap into God's resources our lives will become fruitful, which means that we will produce the fruit of the Spirit as in Galatians 5:22–23 and also that we will bring other people to him.

So, how do we put spiritual roots down into God? We need to stay close. One way is to keep talking with him in prayer, bringing daily concerns, hopes and desires to him. We need to feed on his word, the Bible. What I've found helpful is to learn a verse and then think about it when I get a free moment during the day. Often God will show me ways of making that verse more real in my life so that it is not just buzzing around in my brain, but actually being demonstrated in my attitudes, actions and words throughout the day.

Trusting in my own wisdom and abilities will lead to a barren, parched life. Putting my confidence in God's wisdom and abilities will lead to a beautiful and fruitful life.

CP

Do others have confidence in you?

A wife of noble character who can find? She is worth far more than rubies. Her husband has full confidence in her and lacks nothing of value. She brings him good, not harm, all the days of her life… Charm is deceptive, and beauty is fleeting; but a woman who fears the Lord is to be praised.

As a single person, I have in the past gleefully skipped over Proverbs 31, thinking that it didn't apply to me and I couldn't possibly be that superwoman *par excellence* anyway.

However, I have since learned that it is unwise and even dangerous to ignore portions of God's word, so I thought I'd better take a closer look. The principles in Proverbs 31 can be applied to any relationship—friend, parent, child, as well as spouse.

Do my friends have full confidence in me? Do I support them when others criticize or gossip about them? Can I be trusted with confidences? Do they lack anything of value that I can give them—loyalty, encouragement, prayer support, honesty? Am I willing to confront them when I see them going off track? Do I bring these people good and not harm all the days of my life?

As the years take their toll, it is helpful to be reminded that beauty is fleeting! No amount of creams, potions, pills or exercise programmes can delay the ageing process for ever. Thankfully there is much more to being a woman than just our appearance. Proverbs affirms that praise is to be given to the woman not for her beauty, but for her fear of the Lord. Even though this woman devotes herself to her husband and family, it seems that first place in her life is given to God. Her relationship with God is the source and wellspring of all these beautiful qualities that she brings to her relationships.

Lord, I pray that you would work in my life so that others would have confidence in me and that I would bring them good, not harm, all the days of my life.

CP

Hallo Jesus!

And now, dear children, continue in him, so that when he appears
we may be confident and unashamed before him at his coming...
We know that when he appears, we shall be like him, for we shall
see him as he is.

Jesus is coming back. And he could come today! This time, instead of coming as a vulnerable baby in an insignificant town in Israel, he will come with the deafening trumpet call of God, with blazing fire and powerful angels (1 Thessalonians 4:16; 2 Thessalonians 1:7).

The question for all of us is, will we be confident and unashamed before him at his coming? We know that Jesus has paid the penalty for our sin so that those who trust in him and his work on the cross will be received into heaven (1 Peter 3:18). But when you look at Jesus face to face and see him as he is, will you hang your head or try to hide in a corner? Or will you look up into his glorious face confident and unashamed? Will there be things you will regret? Choices you've made, priorities you've neglected, words you've said, relationship problems that you haven't sought to reconcile?

Two of my aunts had a row and didn't speak for about 25 years. The nearest they got to reconciliation was when one went to the other's funeral. Too late, far too late.

The condition that the apostle John puts on being confident and unashamed before him at his coming is to 'continue in him'. This is a daily walk of faith, seeking to know God better, and not letting anything hurt or hinder that relationship, asking forgiveness as soon as you're conscious of having sinned. This doesn't necessarily mean *doing* more—attending more meetings or exhausting yourself in Christian service. It is a matter of the heart. If your heart is open and tender to God's promptings, then you can be confident and unashamed before him when he returns.

'He who testifies to these things says, "Yes, I am coming soon."
Amen. Come, Lord Jesus' (Revelation 22:20).

CP

The right balance

*But because of the temptation to immorality, each man should
have his own wife, and each woman her own husband. The
husband should give to his wife her conjugal rights, and likewise
the wife to her husband. For the wife does not rule over her own
body, but the husband does; likewise the husband does not rule
over his own body, but the wife does.*

Paul was nothing if not practical about how the Christian faith should work out in people's daily lives. He was a realist—and a revolutionary. He gave women power in marriage that was unheard of in those days. Sadly, Paul's teaching was ignored for centuries, and women continued to be seen as men's property.

So what of sex? The Corinthians had a problem with it. Hardly surprising—the Corinthian Christians had been converted out of a pagan culture in which promiscuous sex was the daily norm. Now they were Christians, they were trying to find a balance between their healthy sexuality and their new faith. Just because they were Christians, it did not mean they had lost their sex drive—far from it.

Paul outlines the Christian way. He assumes that sex is a powerful drive in many people's lives, and nowhere says that this is wrong. Instead, he sets out guidelines on how to channel all this energy.

Paul is no misogynist. He says that women are equal partners in any marriage. Their sexual desires are to be met every bit as much as their husband's. A wife has the God-given right to *enjoy* her husband's body.

'Super-spiritual' partners who make their more 'lusty' partner feel guilty are *not* more spiritual than their partners. Paul says, 'Do not refuse one another.' If you marry, then regular sex is God's will for you.

Roman Catholic moral theologians have puzzled for centuries over the purpose of sexual intercourse within marriage. Paul never even hints that sex should be only for baby-making. Paul takes it for granted that sex happens in marriage because men and women who love each other enjoy it.

Read Song of Solomon.

AC

Remaining single

I wish that all were as I myself am. But each has his own special gift from God, one of one kind and one of another. To the unmarried and the widows, I say that it is well for them to remain single as I do.

Paul might have wished that everyone could remain single, as he did, but nowhere in the Bible does it say that *God* has ever wished this for everyone. Even Paul immediately backs down, and in his very next sentence acknowledges that there are 'horses for courses', and that his calling and gift from God was to singleness.

Out of this reflection come some interesting points for modern women to consider, because Paul goes on to infer that God actively calls some women to a life of singleness. Marriage is *not* the be-all and end-all of life.

I can never understand why people accuse Paul of being a woman-hater. I always think how terrible it would be if he had said the opposite to the unmarried and widows: 'You are a failure, you know, until you marry.' What bondage it would be if a woman was not worth anything until she had succeeded in getting a husband!

Instead, the Bible agrees here with our modern liking for choice in these matters. Women should be able to choose whether to marry or not. They should not be socially penalized if they remain single.

Several of the most productive women I have ever known have been single. They could have married several times over, but such was their calling before God that they decided that they would forgo marriage. The fruitfulness of their lives has been ample proof that for them this was right.

So I welcome Paul's words to the widows and unmarried: 'It is well for them to remain single.' How liberating! They are not bits of unclaimed property, useless until owned by a man. Though single, they are already complete and *doing well*!

The will of God is the measure of things.
AMBROSE

AC

Lifelong commitment

To the married I give charge, not I but the Lord, that the wife should not separate from her husband.

Princess, having had sufficient experience with princes, seeks frog. This is one of many 'bumper stickers' now available for women to put on their cars. Its feisty, no-nonsense attitude towards men will strike a chord in many feminine hearts. For living with a man is often very hard work, and these days women are running out of patience. Statistically, they more often begin divorce proceedings than do men.

But these words from the apostle Paul show that women's desire to bow out of marriage is nothing very new: the women of Corinth two thousand years ago had similar feelings. Paul addresses the main issue behind this problem—the sacred nature of marriage. Marriage, he says, is not something that can be abandoned when you are feeling fed up with your partner. Marriage is a lifelong commitment between you and your husband, underwritten by God himself.

What about when you are a Christian and your husband is not? The Corinthians feared that the unbeliever's lack of faith would harm the believer. But Paul says that, in fact, the opposite is true: 'The unbelieving husband is consecrated through his wife.' Some scholars translate this as 'protected'. If you are a Christian and your husband is not, your faith can still guard and protect him. What a wonderful picture!

Suppose he rejects even this, and deserts you? Paul says that in this case 'the sister is not bound… For God has called us to peace'. But he forbids Christians to leave their non-Christian spouses, challenging them instead with the larger picture: 'Wives, how do you know whether you will save your husband?'

A friend of mine had a husband who was very hostile to Christianity, and openly thought of leaving her because of her Christian faith. My friend did her best not to antagonize her husband, and kept praying. Two years later his hostility has gone. Instead, a gradual spiritual healing is beginning for him. He is even seeking Christian counselling!

Pray for anyone you know whose marriage is under strain.

AC

Called

Only, let every one lead the life which the Lord has assigned to him, and in which God has called him.

When Sir Cliff Richard first became a Christian many years ago, he stopped to re-examine his career. Many of his new Christian friends were urging him to get out of the entertainment business. 'God has other things for you,' they said. Fortunately, a few closer friends, who were also Christian, disagreed. 'God has given you talent in this field,' they said. 'So stay in it.'

Christians, they argued, are not often called to a new occupation. Instead, their old occupation is given new significance. 'Bloom where you are planted' is another popular way of putting it. Most of us feel lost at some point in our lives, wondering if we are really where we should be, and if not, where we should go.

Paul gives Christians some things to bear in mind when considering what to do in their life.

First, be firm and self-confident in your present situation. God knows where you are, and you can serve him right there—even if you are a slave! Paul says,

'There let him remain with God.' So accept your present situation and aim to serve God in it. Accept your responsibilities to others, and don't let them down.

Second, accept your own religious background. If you were raised in a formal Anglican church, sang in a cathedral choir, and are now on a diocesan committee somewhere, you are no more special in the eyes of God than someone who never entered a church before their conversion. Accept the past as past, and look to the future. Outward religion is morally neutral: what matters is our hearts before God.

Third, remember that as Christians we are all one in Christ. Christ makes nonsense of social pecking order between Christians. We have been bought with a price, we are no longer our own: our priority must be to serve him in our present lives with all our hearts, unless he opens other doors for us.

Now commit your day to God.
AC

Look what's coming

Those who marry will have worldly troubles, and I would spare you that. I mean, brethren, the appointed time has grown very short.

I rather like disaster films. *Towering Inferno*, *The Poseidon Adventure*, *Jaws*, *Earthquake*, *Independence Day*, *Titanic*… whether it's fire, tidal waves, sharks, icebergs, earth tremors or unfriendly aliens, I've enjoyed them all—from the safety of my own couch. I've noticed that all these films begin in the same way, with people totally preoccupied with the minutiae of daily life, until—WHAM!—they are swept up in a crisis that shows them their lives in another perspective.

Something like that was happening here. Paul is advising the Corinthians about marriage, and if he sounds negative, it's because he was looking at it against the broader picture.

Remember, this was the time of Nero. The emperor's sanity was unravelling, and degrading persecutions of Jews and Christians had begun. So life was dangerous. Paul had himself been the target of a nasty bit of persecution in Ephesus, the very city he was in as he wrote this letter.

Add to this the destruction of Jerusalem (an event equivalent for us to the destruction of London) and you can see why Paul felt that life was precarious, and that Christians should think hard before taking on more commitments. In fact, Paul writes here almost as if to fellow soldiers fighting a dangerous campaign, deep in enemy territory.

So he lists the events that normally structure our lives—marriage, bereavement, pleasures, possessions, commerce and business—and advises the Corinthians to sit lightly to these daily ties of human life. It was not that marriage and so on were not important, but such were the impending dangers that normal life might soon be swept away.

He was saying in effect, 'The tidal wave is behind us, the iceberg is straight ahead, we're on fire, aliens have landed, and there's a great white shark swimming just underneath you… and you want to plan a summer wedding?'

What preoccupies you? If Jesus came back today, would you be ready?

AC

Date to be announced…

If any one thinks that he is not behaving properly towards his betrothed, if his passions are strong, and it has to be, let him do as he wishes: let them marry—it is no sin.

If, despite all the disasters mentioned yesterday, you still want a summer wedding, Paul says, go ahead.

Have you ever noticed that the people who advocate lengthy engagements are often those who are long-settled in the joys and comfort of marriage themselves? One couple at my old church in London had a very happy marriage with five children, but could not understand why their 21-year-old daughter ever wanted to be alone with her fiancé, and why they didn't want to wait another two years to get married.

It seems that there was a group at Corinth who were also keen on long, chaste relationships—for other people. Paul is writing here to stop them imposing such self-denial on the young couples and making their lives a misery.

Paul did not want the ideal of *self-denial for its own sake* to become the supreme virtue in the Corinthian church. While some Corinthians had reacted in this way to the promiscuity all around them, still abstinence from sex was not God's will for everyone either. But neither was Paul prepared to accept a free-and-easy approach to sex. So he stresses the right way, the way that God has laid down for couples.

- Waiting does not get you any moral credit. If you want to marry, marry. Self-denial over this is pointless. God blesses marriage—get on with it!
- If, however, you both wish to wait for good reasons, and are both happy to do so, then so be it. Don't let anyone push you into marriage before you are ready.

The main point for Paul is that *neither* engaged couples who wait *nor* engaged couples who marry quickly risk missing God's best for them. It is a choice up to the individuals involved, to make with each other and before God.

Pray for any couple you know preparing for marriage.

AC

119

Old dogs… new tricks?

If the husband dies, she is free to be married to whom she wishes, only in the Lord. But in my judgment she is happier if she remains as she is.

These verses should be read with Paul's other advice to widows in mind. When writing to Timothy, he urged that younger widows should be encouraged to remarry and have children. To Paul, a real 'widow' was 'not less than 60 years of age'. So it seems to me that in today's reading he was writing with at least middle-aged women in mind.

A woman who has lost a husband after many years faces a major adjustment. No more easy daily companionship, no one to 'protect' her in awkward situations. She becomes socially invisible. Suddenly it is just her against the world. A daunting prospect—so it's easy to understand the temptation to plunge into another marriage, just for the company.

A friend of mine was widowed suddenly at 59. Within months the local widowers were coming out of the woodwork and beating a path to her door. At first they wanted to talk, to take her for meals. Soon they wanted *her* to cook meals for *them*, and listen to all *their* problems…

My friend was a canny woman. She thought long and hard. She decided that middle-aged men (at least the ones she met) did not come problem-free. Instead, they seemed to carry a lot of debris from their own past lives. Did she really want to take on 'an old dog' and face either living with his bad habits or trying to teach him new tricks?

So she took Paul's advice, and it has worked: eighteen years later, she is a *very happy* widow. Now 77, she has dozens of friends and a social life that would wear out many teenagers.

Of course, true love can be found a second time. Just make sure that it is love, not loneliness.

Pray for anyone you know who has been recently widowed.

AC

God and music

My heart is steadfast, O God; I will sing and make music with all my soul.

When I was thinking about a theme for these ten days' readings, I kept coming back not to the notion of *a* theme—but to the use of the word in music, as in a group of notes forming a recognizable tune. I know little about music: the theory of it has always been too much for me to comprehend, so why should I even contemplate writing about it? As Charles Lamb said, 'Sentimentally I am disposed to harmony—but organically I am incapable of a tune!' (*Essays of Elia*).

Yet despite this total lack of knowledge, I adore music. I have been touched by pieces of music and songs that have moved me, thrilled me, challenged me and spurred me on! In many ways God and music go together well in my life, as much of what he does is a mystery to me. I don't understand how he does the things he does, but his work—his 'music'—in my life touches and challenges me. He draws alongside and invites me to listen to his tune, his song, and when I'm ready to join in, my life and his are lived in harmony.

Music is part of creation. It is God's invention, part of his unique creative work which is evident each and every day. From bird-song to whale-song, from the highest heavens to the depths of the oceans, creation sings to God. Joel Edwards rightly says that 'creation is a symphony of harmonizing differences'.

What about us? Our lives may feel and sound like battered old tunes sometimes. What tunes do we sing, what melody can be heard within our lives? We do have a part to play—our own unique song to sing in time and in tune with his.

Dear Father, sometimes my life seems out of tune with your purposes. Draw me close to hear your song—to know that 'it is well with my soul'.

SW

Where we sing

*About midnight Paul and Silas were praying and singing hymns
to God, and the other prisoners were listening to them.*

This is a familiar scripture. I have often wondered what I would do in such a situation. Would I be praying and singing hymns at midnight if I were locked up in prison? With my voice, I wouldn't be allowed to sing at all!

Some time ago I read of a Christian lady, Madame Guyon, falsely imprisoned during the French Revolution. In 1688 she wrote a poem likening her imprisonment to a bird shut away in a cage, unable to fly:

*Naught have I else to do.
I sing the whole day long
And he whom most I love to
                              please
Doth listen to my song.
He caught and bound my
                       wandering wing
But still he bends to hear me sing.*

*My cage confines me all around,
Abroad I cannot flee,
But though my wing is closely
                                 bound
My heart's at liberty.
My prison walls cannot control
The liberty of my soul.*

There are other types of 'prisons' that we may encounter throughout our lives. Sometimes we are prisoners of circumstance and find ourselves locked in situations out of our control and wonder what on earth we have done to deserve all that we face. When I first read this poem, I was tussling with the decision to use a wheelchair. To me it seemed as if a cage had confined me. My wings had been well and truly clipped. Yet despite the confines and constraints, I began to realize that no prison of circumstance or illness can control the liberty of my soul.

Prison is a horrible place—as it is intended to be. To be wrongly imprisoned must be nightmarish. Thank God, many of us will never experience it—but when we do experience 'circumstantial prisons', what hymns and songs do we sing? Is it possible to sing at all? I know that it is… he knows that I do!

'He leads forth the prisoners with singing' (Psalm 68:6). Amen!
                                                        SW

When we sing

I thought about the former days, the years of long ago. I
remembered my songs in the night. My heart mused.

Many may have experienced such turmoil and tragedy that sleep seems to vanish. In my experience it is at those times that God draws close, something within responds and a song in the night is born.

There is something about the night that hones our senses. Towards the end of my Student Nurse training, I was on night duty on the gynaecology ward. It was the blazing hot summer of 1976 so I hadn't slept much and the shift was to be a busy one. One patient, Billie, had been with us for weeks. She had been diagnosed with a very rare ovarian cancer and, despite every treatment, she was dying. She had the most beautiful singing voice and would keep the other ladies entertained with her songs. During the night we had an emergency admission—a lady giving birth despite being only six months pregnant. The baby arrived before the doctor could, and was stillborn. I was alone with her and we wept as I held her and her child.

As she was transferred to theatre, I went to check on the other patients, as the noise and the clatter would have disturbed them. There was only the sound of Billie's voice singing softly—a song in the night. In the dark I listened, as transfixed as the other ladies were. I was standing between life and death, triumph and tragedy. I had held someone in my arms who hadn't survived and now I was listening to a lady with such strength of will that, despite all that she faced, she could keep on singing. Three weeks later she died.

And now I sing my own song in the night, aware that God is with me, listening.

Father God, in the dark night of the soul, let our songs of the night come to you. Amen.

SW

What we sing

Consider the voice of the singers at the watering places. They recite the righteous acts of the Lord.

Centuries ago, minstrels travelled the land, singing songs of battles in the Crusades. They also communicated news from village to village or expressed the love of one to another. In today's passage of scripture, the singers tell of the righteous acts of the Lord and bring encouragement to their listeners.

Our 'watering places' have taken on a different guise—we gather as the Church—but the message can still be the same and the songs we sing can still have a profound effect on those who listen. Apparently, in the 16th century Martin Luther won as many converts to Christ through his encouragement of congregational singing as he did through preaching. Also, in the 18th century, for every person won to Christ through the Wesleys' preaching, ten were won through their music. Something deep within us responds to God in music.

When I became a Christian, I attended a charismatic church. The songs and hymns were sung at a cracking pace, and with such feeling and fervour, we would often still be there at 10pm! I still have the old *Redemption Hymnal* and love to look through it at such hymns as 'Blessed Assurance' and 'Love Divine'. These days our gaze has shifted from a dusty old hymn book to the glare of the OHP screen. Yet those songs and hymns still stir something within me—so much so that I still sing them in the shower or even wake up with the tune of one of them buzzing around my head.

Fashions change but the Church still needs to be that watering place where people can come to hear us 'recite the righteous acts of the Lord' in a style and manner that is both challenging and relevant. Yet there remains a place for some of the hymns that have stood the test of time: they may be old, but they can be ever new!

Amazing grace! How sweet the sound that saved a wretch like me.

JOHN NEWTON (1725–1807)

SW

How we sing

*Sing joyfully to the Lord, you righteous… Sing to him a new
song; play skilfully, and shout for joy.*

What about those who find it almost impossible to hold a tune? It is just as well that I live alone as my singing has been likened to the death throes of an animal in distress!

At school I did try to learn to play the recorder—who didn't? My problem was that I couldn't read music, so rather than read the score I would try to copy what others were doing on their recorders—total mayhem on the ear, as I was always one note behind!

So if our singing is distressing for others and playing an instrument more so, what do we do? I *listen.* My collection of CDs ranges from classical and opera to folk and blues, to jazz and pop, to the Vineyard and Hillsong classics. I love to listen to music. I'm so grateful to a music teacher who quickly recognized where my talents lay—as far away from instruments and singing as possible, but close to a record player. He introduced me to Grieg, Holst and others, and we became firm friends.

Years later I had the opportunity to see the London Symphony Orchestra perform, and was thrilled as I 'saw' music being made. Each musician had a copy of the score; each played a particular instrument; each looked at the conductor to lead them through the music. They played when beckoned, all the while keeping their eyes on the score and on him. Even the tiniest of instruments was important for the symphony to be played well.

That evening I saw a wonderful illustration of the Church. Each of us has our 'score' bearing its own unique tune; each of us is ready to play as our heavenly conductor beckons: whether we are trumpets or triangles, we have a part to play. The symphony just wouldn't sound the same without each one of us.

Father, whether we sing, shout, or play skilfully, let our lives be in harmony with you and others.

SW

The Hallelujah Chorus

Then I heard what sounded like a great multitude… shouting:
'Hallelujah! For our Lord God Almighty reigns!'

Heaven's anthem—one day, when we are gathered before the Lord, this shall indeed be our song! I long for that day.

In 1997 I had the opportunity for a 'rehearsal'… and almost blew it! Some may be familiar with the 'Voices for Hospices' events that have been held worldwide. The idea is to raise money for the hospice movement and to have a 24-hour 'Hallelujah' ringing around the globe. Some friends from church were part of the event in Newcastle. I had the audacity to ask to join them.

Prior to the event I had borrowed a recording of Handel's *Messiah* and a score. I listened—but couldn't follow the score. But I knew that as long as I was next to someone who *could* sing, I could keep up, almost in tune! My friend Jan has the most wonderful soprano voice and offered to let me sit next to her. We gathered at the cathedral. There was a formidable gathering of choirs familiar with *Messiah*. My wheelchair and I were parked in the centre aisle and we rehearsed everything *but* the Hallelujah Chorus. I had been able to keep up—at least Jan knew when to turn the pages of the score at the right time.

The actual performance started with hundreds of others around the country. Finally, the Hallelujah Chorus—expectancy heightened! I headed off with the others towards the final crescendo when I noticed that those around me were giggling and crying, unable to keep up! Was my singing that awful, I wondered. But no, it was because I had decided to sing every 'Hallelujah' I possibly could, from soprano to bass. I was singing with every fibre of my being. No wonder they giggled—perhaps God did too!

That was some practice run for the day when I will be with that multitude in heaven and shall once again sing, with all my being, my Hallelujahs to God!

Father, one day I shall see you face to face. Hallelujah!

SW

A plaintive song of the exile

How can we sing the songs of the Lord while in a foreign land?

This psalm speaks about the enforced exile of the people of Israel to Babylon—seventy years of misery in a foreign land. How could they possibly sing for their tormentors?

Am I the only one who finds it difficult at times to sing the songs of Zion? I do often feel out of tune with those around me, as my life has shifted into a minor key. The tune is there, it is just a little slower and more melancholic.

Despite my lack of theoretical knowledge of music I know that in any piece there are minor chords that bring a depth and resonance to the tune. Sometimes it is the plaintive song of the exile that touches the heart of God. Through no fault of our own we feel exiled and as if we inhabit a strange land—out of tune with those around us. Our lives are turned upside down by circumstance.

I heard recently that Rachmaninov, in his 'Variations on a Theme of Paganini', took Paganini's tune (familiar to some as the theme to 'The South Bank Show') and turned it upside down to create the sublime 18th Variation, which I love. If Rachmaninov could do that with a piece of music, what can God do with our lives when they have been turned upside down? What a melody we can still produce by the grace of God: life in a minor key is still valid and valued by God. Sometimes our songs from exile, or indeed our songs in the night, have no audience. No one hears. Yet we do have an audience with the King of kings whose ear is open to our plaintive song.

Blessed assurance,
Jesus is mine…
This is my story,
this is my song—
Praising my Saviour
all the day long.
FANNY J. CROSBY (1820–1915)

SW

Strung out!

If musical instruments, flutes or harps—aren't played so that each note is distinct and in tune, how will anyone be able to catch the melody and enjoy the music?

I am a listener *to* and not a player *of* any instrument and yet many times in the Bible, reference is given to playing and being an 'instrument' for God. We do have a part to play—in tune with his purposes.

But what of those times when music is the last thing on our minds, and being aware of the part we play seems a distant dream? We are strung out—pulled in all directions—and something within us snaps.

Nicolo Paganini was a gifted violinist, and a colourful showman. During a performance of a difficult piece of music, one string on his violin snapped. He frowned but continued to play and improvise. To the surprise of the conductor of the orchestra, a second string broke, and then a third! Three limp strings dangled from Paganini's violin, but he continued to play on the one remaining string. The audience erupted in loud applause as he held his violin high for everyone to see, and with a twinkle in his eye he smiled and said 'Paganini... and one string!'

Sometimes we may feel that we are unable to play a note, let alone make the tunes of our lives distinctive to those around us. Situations and circumstances can snap even the strongest of us. The 'strings' of our lives may hang limp and useless. I wonder if Paul felt like that as he languished in prison, alone. Or even Jesus as he hung on the cross, deserted and rejected. Even with one string our lives can make a difference, because we keep on believing, keep on trusting and hoping. The tune is still played and the melody is heard. Paganini and one string —*your life* and one string. That's all it takes.

Dear Father, sometimes the strings in our lives hang limp and lifeless—yet help us to do what we can with what we have.
SW

The therapy of music

*David would take his harp and play. Then relief would come to
Saul; he would feel better, and the evil spirit would leave him.*

Saul had been rejected by God—
1 Samuel 15 tells the story. He
was a tormented individual,
given to bouts of despondency,
jealousy and violence. A life that
held such promise fell apart. At
those times when Saul was most
aggravated and agitated, David
the psalmist would play his harp
for him and peace would come.

This is a wonderful illustration of the therapeutic effects
that music can have upon our
lives: even Elisha used music to
help him to receive the word of
the Lord (2 Kings 3:15).

It has long been noted that
music can have a positive effect
upon us. 'Music hath charms to
soothe a savage breast' (William
Congreve, 'The Mourning Bride').
Apparently, if babies hear music
whilst still in the womb, they
often respond to it once they are
born—amazing!

I often have times when I use
music to calm me after a difficult
day. The music and the words
wash over me and I am stilled
before God.

One particular song did just
that for me years ago. I was
returning home from work—the
last time I would return to that
particular home. I had to sell it,
as walking and stair-climbing
were becoming a problem for me
as a wheelchair user. A hymn
started to play through the car
cassette: 'Be still my soul… the
Lord is on thy side'. I stopped the
car and listened. Each verse
seemed to have something to say
to me that day: in every change
he faithful would remain—he
would guide my future as he had
the past. Into my gaping unknown he would come—and he
did.

I love that hymn and it continues to bring comfort and
encouragement to my life.
Perhaps you too have a song or
some music that touches you and
soothes your troubles.

---

*Be still my soul—the waves and
winds still know his voice who
ruled them while he dwelt below.*
KATHERINA A.D. VON SCHLEGEL, 1752
(TRS. JANE L. BORTHWICK, 1855)

SW

The sound of silence

When he opened the seventh seal, there was silence in heaven for about half an hour.

In Revelation 5 it says that thousands upon thousands of angels encircle the throne of God and sing 'Worthy is the Lamb'. I do find it difficult to picture what heaven will be like. In other chapters we are given a glimpse of the sound of multitudes singing songs of endless praise.

Yet for a brief time we read of silence in heaven—no singing, not a sound—silence.

Not everything in music is audible. Silence is as much a part of music as the squiggly notes on the page. Perhaps at last I have found my part—I can 'sing' the silences!

It isn't often that we are completely surrounded by silence: creation can be incredibly noisy. Take time to listen and try not to hear the noise.

A few weeks ago I met a lady who is struggling to come to terms with her hearing loss. She feels hemmed in by silence and misunderstanding, alone and isolated by an impairment few of us really understand. Added to that is the knowledge that her impairment is genetic and has

been passed on to her two little boys. She asked me one question: 'Where is God?' I floundered to give her an answer. Was it sufficient to say, 'He's here'? It was all that I could say because it was all that I knew. The God who so wonderfully created the sounds of creation also created the silence too. He who made the music of bird-song can also make himself heard above the turmoil of war, and through the silence of death. When God speaks, it isn't often audible.

I don't know why God allows little boys to lose their hearing or why their mum suffers as she struggles to make sense out of it all. All I know is that he will speak with her somehow with his unmistakable still, small voice. I just know he will.

Speak even in the silence, Lord. Amen.

                                    SW

DAY
BY
DAY
WITH
GOD

MAGAZINE SECTION

Making things work	132
The meaning of mothering	135
Food for thought	138
For his name's sake	142
Still Time for Eternity	145
Other Christina Press titles	152
Other BRF titles	154
Order forms	156
Subscription information	158

Making things work

Chris Leonard

I'd been especially looking forward to this Writers' Day in London—and not only because of the exceptional speakers. Having finished a five-year term on the committee of the organization running the event, I no longer had any responsibility for 'making things work'!

The hall filled with hundreds of eager writers expecting a brilliant day. Susan Howatch was speaking, plus Mark LeFanu from the Society of Authors, Andrew Taylor the crime writer, and Paul Handley who edits the *Church Times*. Shortly before the programme was due to start, I spotted the Chairman looking worried, and asked if I could help. 'The PA's not working,' she said. Together we stared at the complicated stack of equipment. Speaking into all four microphones made little green lights dance prettily on the display panel but no sound emerged from the loudspeakers. We twiddled knobs, pressed switches, slid sliders and checked plugs; we laid hands on the stack and prayed. Others joined us in vain. We phoned two clued-up husbands, but their advice led us nowhere.

Problem

Someone bellowed, 'We have a problem. Does anyone know how to make PA systems work?' But the hall was full of writers, and one thing I learnt while on the committee was that, in distributing gifts, God seldom gives writing and practical abilities to the same people. I, for example, rely on my husband with absolute faith. If anything doesn't work, whether mechanical, electrical or computerized, John will understand and fix it. Our children, friends, neighbours and church all have similar faith in him, poor man. But though I've watched him 'make PAs work' many times and although he's tried to explain it all to me, I remain utterly clueless. I called him on the mobile.

John had travelled up to London with me, intending to do some shopping and to visit the National Gallery. Now he hared over to the hall through heavy rain. I just knew that the minute he arrived he'd spot some muting control or loose connection that we had missed. Recognizing who was boss, the PA would magically work again.

Not so. At first we amateurs rejoiced in not having been proved stupid. Then we worried. By this time, the event's programme had started. A trained singer, who wouldn't have needed amplification to make announcements at Waterloo station, welcomed everyone, then led some worship. But we could hardly assume such astounding voice production from our guest speakers.

Meanwhile my husband pronounced, in a whisper, 'This stack may look complete but there's no way anything in it powers the loudspeakers.' Oh. So where was the switch? Nowhere obvious. Yet at his words a penny dropped, not so much in my brain as in my sub-conscious. Six months before, while suffering overload at the end of teaching a course in this very building, hadn't I been shown a switch? Because PA was never my responsibility, I'd not expected to need the information again. My feet, rather than my brain, led me forward.

'This way!' I said, and four surprised people followed me up the side of the building, through a seminar room, ante-room and then an office. Beyond that I opened a door, announcing, 'The switch is in here!' Within seconds John had located it amid a mass of wires, and the PA, whose sliders had been left at full volume, started producing excruciating noises. Running back to the controls, he soon had the situation sorted, the first of the day's speakers was only marginally inconvenienced and a great time was enjoyed by all.

Prayer

The moral? That God often makes us, in unexpected ways, the answer to our own prayers. And that the dashing around I do—we do—to 'make things work', whether it's about electrical equipment, helping others, organizing meetings or cooking the family's dinner, may go to waste unless we're switched on to the source of real power. It's all too easy to forget about that. I know, because I'd forgotten it again only two days later.

That evening I was due to lead a group in our home discussing issues concerning the misuse of control and authority. I'd worked hard beforehand to ensure that everything was under control. I'd organized a lift for an elderly member of the group, made the house and myself reasonably clean and tidy, put the coffee and chairs ready, prepared the discussion, cooked the family's meal, completed my e-mails, answered complicated A/S level homework questions, said prayers, fed rabbit, sorted son arriving home from agricultural college after rain-soaked sheep practical… and then the same son made a clumsy movement during the meal which (to my over-wrought thinking) nearly wrecked my computer and desk. I yelled at him in a remarkably ineffective and damaging attempt to restore order. I ended up leading the discussion on how to 'make things work' in the area of authority, while feeling a complete prune.

So how *do* you make things work? Looking back over my notes from that Writers' Day, something that Susan Howatch said caught my eye. She talked about the attractive alternative lifestyle of Christians, which isn't selfish. It's not about doing what society wants or what others think we should. No, it's about *following the path God wants for each of us as he makes his creation come right*. Re-reading that, another penny dropped. We're to help things to work, not on our own, but as part of his team, playing to his game-plan and rules. We're to let him take the burden of responsibility and find in him, not in ourselves, the power to do what he asks. We're to take time to find him in the still centre of the whirlwind of our activities. Help us all to remember that, Lord, when we audaciously try to 'make things work' for you!

The meaning of mothering

Margaret Killingray

I am very glad that the Sunday when we remember mothers is called Mothering Sunday. I am glad because it helps me not just to remember the fact that I had a mother and to thank the Lord for her balanced, easy-to-live-with kind of love, but also to think about what 'mothering' means. Thinking about that opens up all the passages in the Bible which tell us that God is like a parent to us—a father who mothers us!

This makes me realize how much we do need to sort out what these very common, very ordinary words mean, where today 'fathering' sometimes implies just the act of conceiving a child, and 'mothering' inplies warm, cuddling—even smothering—love.

I asked a fidgeting huddle of primary-age children in church one morning what they would like their mothers to let them do today. They giggled and vied with each other in being outrageous. Their answers included eating chocolate for breakfast; staying in bed and not going to school; never having a bath; staying up late and watching videos; spending more time on the Playstation; playing with real tools; and, from my grandson, playing with electricity!

Our need

I did get those children, reluctantly, to admit that mothers who gave them everything they wanted might not be such a good idea after a while. I wanted them to think about the kind of mothering they and all human beings need, and who can deliver such mothering.

Many of us are haunted by images of unmothered children—in the orphanages of eastern Europe, for example. At the other end of the scale, we may know personally of those whose adult lives are distorted by the overwhelming, smothering mothering they had as children. What is good mothering?

There is a passage in Hosea 11 where the prophet tells us that God says to his people, 'I loved you like a mother, but you have disobeyed me and now, although I still love you with passion, you will have to accept the consequences of what you have done. But I still love you, and if you come back you will know my warm, forgiving love again.'

In the story Jesus told of the prodigal son and the waiting father, the father loves his son, but lets him leave—lets him go in disobedience to suffer the consequences of his waywardness. But he waits in love until the son comes back to find mothering, forgiving love again. This message comes over and over again in many different forms in the Bible. God loves us and showers all his blessing and grace upon us, but he does not smother us. He allows us the freedom to disobey. He does not compel, nor does he blackmail us, but waits for our return, to find that the full glory of his love has been there all the time.

This is God's treatment of us, and here we learn the shape of true mothering, true parenting. All children need mothering that makes them feel good, that recognizes each child's unique importance, that tells them they matter and are appreciated, that makes bad things better, that physically cuddles and holds.

Letting go
But children also need mothering that allows them to learn, even by their mistakes; helps them to try harder, do better, learn self-discipline—even for chocolate, bathing and television; sometimes disciplines and allows painful consequences to take their course. True mothering also means letting go—at the right time, preferably, but sometimes when they insist, even though it will not do them any good.

There are two kinds of mothering—a warm, 'cuddling', totally accepting love and a strong, discipling—and disciplining—love, both of which we all need in order to have the best chance of growing into well-rounded adulthood. They are needed by children above all, but, just as we all need the mothering love of God all our lives, so we need to have that love mediated to us by others all our lives.

So in one sense we all need mothering—by fathers and mothers, by teachers and bosses, by friends and neighbours, in both these ways at different times. And all of us who have learnt the nature of mothering from our earliest memories are able to respond in motherly ways when that response is needed by others.

We are, by definition as humans, children who are loved but children who disobey. If we have been mothered well, and can today thank our mothers, fathers and many others for that, then we will understand that we probably have to make the first move and seek God's forgiving, warm love for ourselves. Meanwhile, who needs your mothering most at the moment?

Food for thought

Alie Stibbe

Jesus said, 'Make a tree good and its fruit will be good, or make a tree bad and its fruit will be bad, for a tree is recognized by its fruit… The good man brings good things out of the good stored up in him, and the evil man brings evil things out of the evil stored up in him' (Matthew 12:33, 35, NIV).

I have recently cut down and burnt an unproductive apple tree and replaced it with four new saplings. These young trees won't be left to grow in any direction they like: they have been staked up and fed the right plant food. The lower branches have been correctly pruned, and when the main stem reaches the right height, the growing point will be cut out. Each year the trees will get the food they need, so that they produce healthy fruit when they reach maturity.

There is not much difference between trees and children! Children need support, to be fed properly and directed in the ways that they should develop. Then, watered with love and prayer, they should grow up to stand upright before the Lord and continue in the way you have taught them (Proverbs 22:6).

Today's culture

'Raise a child to love the Lord' inevitably sounds quite directive, and in that respect Christian parenting runs up against the brick wall of modern secular thought. Today we live in a culture where the child is central: its needs must be met and whims obeyed. This is not a scriptural principle. In Ephesians 6:1 we read that children are to obey their parents in the Lord. The idea that children should be obedient indicates that parents are to be directive, give support and make decisions on the child's behalf until they are old enough to do this for themselves—although Paul does warn parents not to exasperate their children!

Children need immense support in the current cultural environment in relation to the media, including TV, magazines, CDs, tapes, CD-roms, videos, computer games, films, books, music, and the

Internet. My main concern in this area is not only its content, but also the apparent ignorance that some Christian parents seem to show about what the Bible says is a suitable choice of 'food' for our children from the secular smorgasbord.

None of us would deliberately give our children something bad to read or watch (Luke 11:11–12). But sometimes our children do get what is less than nourishing because we don't realize that a thing is packed with junk—the label looked acceptable and we haven't had time to check what's inside the wrapper. It is essential to take time to check what our children are reading, watching and playing with, at home and elsewhere.

Most of us would agree that the Bible makes it very clear that we should stay clear of sexual sin and anything that leads us to be tempted to wrong thoughts, desires and actions (Galatians 5: 19–21). We would not give our children unsuitable reading matter or allow them to watch anything with overt sexual content on the TV or at the cinema, or get involved in an inadvisable relationship.

Pop lyrics

Having said that, it is unbelievable what our children find to feed on without us even realizing. I caught the lyrics of one of the pop songs my son had taped from the radio, as he played it to a car full of teenagers on the drive to school one morning. I think he was more taken up with the tune than the mumbled words, but this incident began an interesting discussion about how Christians should conduct relationships.

TV has been an ongoing area of discussion with our children ever since they discovered the 'on' switch. They know that we don't want them watching certain programmes and are very careful to change channels or switch off when these shows begin. Thankfully our children don't yet watch anything after the 9pm watershed, but I am more concerned about their exposure to the supernatural themes that have crept into children's broadcasting.

I studied a TV schedule recently and discovered that all but one show on one children's cable channel had supernatural content. About half of another's were similar, as was the teenage channel. The scattering of Japanese occult-based *animé* being broadcast across all the children's channels made it tempting to reduce our subscription to sports and wildlife documentaries alone.

Children's books

Another area where the fascination with the supernatural has taken a hold is that of children's books. Once children start to read, their minds can be assaulted by undesirable stories and ideas that do not conform to the pure, lovely, noble, true, right and admirable qualities that Paul encourages us to fix our minds upon (Philippians 4:8–10).

Early exposure to such stories builds up a subconscious fascination with the supernatural that entices children to read more blatantly unsuitable books when they get older. And 'older' does not mean 'teenage'. Horror and occult books are now freely available to any child that can read. When we think about things that are 'lovely, pure and true', we are promised that the peace of God will be with us (Philippians 4:9). If our minds, or our children's minds, are filled with stories of fear, blood and supernatural ooze, there will not be much peace in their hearts or minds. Children who read such books could have disturbed sleep.

Although Paul lists witchcraft and idolatry alongside sexual immorality in a list of things to be avoided (Galatians 5:16–17), some parents don't take this issue seriously. They seem unaware that fascination and involvement with the supernatural is dangerous and that God forbids us to have anything to do with it (Leviticus 19:31; Ephesians 5:11–16). There are several reasons for this:

- We have been deceived by the lies of the devil (Ephesians 6:11; 2 Corinthians 2:11).

- We do not read the Bible enough and therefore do not know what God has to say about the dangers of flirting with the supernatural.

- Christian leaders need encouragement to speak on this subject, not to be fearful (Joshua 1:5–9) and to stand firm on what they know is right (2 Thessalonians 2:15).

- We are influenced by a free-thinking society that advocates the 'I'll do it my way' principle, and are unwilling to listen to leaders who do speak out (Hebrews 13:17).

- We do not listen to the Holy Spirit within us (John 16:13).

Never too late...

What our children absorb directly or passively will affect the sort of people they become. Don't be afraid to train children in the way they should go. Never think that it is too late: with love, time and patience, young trees can be persuaded to straighten out and produce healthy fruit. The same applies to raising healthy children. To ensure this, we need to walk in the Spirit, listen to his promptings, search the scriptures, be obedient and live a consistent life as an example to the next generation.

For his name's sake

Beryl Adamsbaum

'Why don't you take a stroll through Psalm 23?' was a suggestion made to me during a painful time of re-examination and inner turmoil. 'And I'll follow you with my prayers.' Little did I know, when I embarked upon my walk, where the way would lead me!

Psalm 23 has often been a lifeline to me in times of trouble. Reciting it slowly and meditatively during sleepless stretches of the night has restored peace and calm to my agitated soul and given me the longed-for rest. This time, however, before making me 'lie down in green pastures', the Shepherd took me along a different track. I sat up, alert, as I read, 'He guides me in paths of righteousness for his name's sake.' That little phrase, 'for his name's sake', caused me to stop and think. First of all, what does it mean? And then, if it is 'for his name's sake' that 'he guides me in paths of righteousness', maybe everything else he does is 'for his name's sake' as well? So, perhaps that should be my focus too?

The importance of a name

'For his name's sake'—one of those phrases we almost take for granted. We read or hear these four words from time to time, tacked on to one statement or another, without even thinking about the meaning of them. We know that the scriptures attach much more importance to a name than we do here in Western Europe, though some countries and cultures of the world do still choose names weighty with meaning for their children. Names in the Bible, however, are often expressions of the very character and nature of those who own them. The name is in fact the equivalent of the person. So in that short, seemingly insignificant phrase, 'for his name's sake', we see that God's character, and therefore his reputation, is at stake. And if he leads us in 'paths of righteousness' or 'right paths', it is so that his name will be vindicated. What we do and are reflects on God. If we profess to be his children—the sheep belonging to the

Shepherd, to keep the imagery of Psalm 23—then the way we behave is not just our own business (as we may sometimes, mistakenly, think it is—autonomous, independent creatures that we tend to want to be), our conduct is a reflection on the Shepherd we profess to follow. 'He guides us in paths of righteousness for his name's sake.' The way we walk, if we follow his leading along the right paths, will reflect on him and bring him honour. Conversely, if we choose to take wrong paths, we will bring shame upon him—upon his name, his character, his person.

God has much to say about his name in the instructions he gives to his prophet Ezekiel. This helps us to understand the reference in Psalm 23. In Ezekiel 36:22, God tells his prophet to 'say to the house of Israel, "This is what the sovereign Lord says: It is not for your sake, O house of Israel, that I am going to do these things, but for the sake of my holy name… Then the nations will know that I am the Lord".' He then proceeds to tell Ezekiel, in the following verses, exactly what blessings he is going to pour out upon his people, and he says again, 'I want you to know that I am not doing this for your sake… Then the nations around you that remain will know that I the Lord have rebuilt what was destroyed and have replanted what was desolate… Then they will know that I am the Lord' (Ezekiel 36:32, 36, 38). It was 'for his name's sake'.

A bigger perspective

'He guides me in paths of righteousness' not primarily for my own good, my own comfort, my own protection (though these are all by-products of his leading), but rather 'for his name's sake'. Similarly, all he gave to his people—the redemption, cleansing, forgiveness and salvation, as well as the material blessings such as food and houses, recorded for us in Ezekiel 36—was not primarily for their own advantage, even though they benefited greatly, but 'for the sake of [his] holy name'. Psalm 106:8 perhaps gives us a clearer understanding of this. We read that God saved his people 'for his name's sake, to make his mighty power known'. This gives us a much bigger perspective on life.

The preoccupation with God's 'name' will also affect our praying. Why do I pray? What do I pray for? When I pray, is it 'for his name's sake' or for the sake of my own advancement and gratification? What is the aim of my praying? The glory of God, or the well-being of humankind? As we have seen in the book of the prophet Ezekiel, the two often go together: God is glorified through what he does for his children. But what is our focus—God's glory, or the fulfilment of our needs or, even worse, of our selfish desires? James says in his letter, 'When you ask, you do not receive, because you ask with wrong motives, that you may spend what you get on your pleasures' (James 4:3). And when we look at the world at large, with all the conflict, persecution, famine and natural disasters, do we pray that God will intervene and act 'for his name's sake'—for his honour and glory? When we pray for missionaries in far-off lands, do we stop at their own comfort and well-being, or do we pray that God might be glorified through the blessings we ask him to shower upon them, so that he might be revealed to the surrounding nations?

Refreshment and restoration

My 'stroll through Psalm 23' was not the peaceful meander I expected it to be! Seeking refreshment and restoration for my own soul, I was pulled up short by an encounter with the Good Shepherd, the one who laid down his life for the sheep who listen to his voice and follow him (John 10:11, 27, 28). My focus—which at that time was on myself and my problems, on my pain and weariness—changed dramatically as I began to ask myself the above questions. At first my thoughts were in confusion. I no longer knew how to pray. I was faced with my own selfishness. I was obliged to question my motives, to examine my desires, to search my heart. But soon, with the words of the apostle John ringing in my ears—'Your sins are forgiven you *for his name's sake*' (1 John 2:12, AV)—I took courage and walked out of the dark valley and into the green pastures.

Still Time for Eternity

Margaret Cundiff writes:

The experiences of living through a particular period of time can provide us not only with something to look back on, but give us an incentive to go forward. During the winding up of the 20th century and the beginning of the 21st, there have been times when it has seemed that the world in general, and my own personal world, have stood still for a few moments, long enough to give time to see the bigger picture, the larger world, the working out of God's kingdom here on earth in the context of eternity. It is like a series of photographs which enable us to relive certain moments, reflect on them and, by taking a closer look, see if there is more to them than met our eye or took our attention when we looked through the view-finder and pressed the button. This book is a series of such snapshots, set in the frame of God's word. I realize that other people's holiday snaps can be boring, but I hope you will enjoy sharing some of my stills of a very special period in history, and that they will encourage you to take a fresh look at some of your own, and share them with others—moments of time, captured in the heart, worth a second look before we all dash on. After all, there is still time for eternity, and isn't that what really matters?

You can find further details of this book on page 154, and an order form on page 157. Alternatively, *Still Time for Eternity* is available from your local Christian bookshop.

COME FLY WITH ME

My birthday was hovering on the near horizon, the annual addition to the tally of years, causing for my nearest and dearest the problem of how to reward me for such a noteworthy achievement. Most surprises had been tried over the years, with varying success, but nowadays, or nowayears, the ball was put into my court and batted to and fro until some sort of a solution was found—and, I may say, always enjoyed and appreciated. So the inevitable question was tossed casually my way. 'What would you like for your birthday?' I could see from Peter's glazed expression that he was already running through the usual list of smellies, something from the underwear department of a well-known chain store, a CD or tape, maybe a book or magazine subscription, the usual sort of thing. So when I said, 'A kite', it rather threw him.

I saw him do a double take and then he repeated what I had said, slowly with a suspicious note. 'A kite?'

'Yes, a kite.'

'A kite? What do you want a kite for?' A silly question, I thought, surely everyone knows what you do with a kite.

'I want a kite to fly it, that's what you do with kites.'

He seemed to get the general idea. 'But why do you want one?'

Patiently I explained that I had wanted a kite for a long time, it was one of those things that had been on my 'one day I will' list, but now the time was right. Well, at least I had decided it was.

Peter gave in. 'And where do you get kites from?' This I had worked out. I knew exactly the place. In fact, I knew the range of kites stocked, because I had spent some time studying them, and would quite happily have any of them—as a starter, of course, but that detail could be kept for later.

End of conversation, and I did half wonder whether he had taken me seriously. But then, after all these years of knowing me, I felt he knew when I really meant what I said, however strange it might seem. And on my birthday, sure enough, there it was—my kite.

A few days later, with the wind blowing at just the right speed, the kite got its first outing. It took to the air as to the manner born (or manufactured), a joy to behold and hold and direct and marvel at; and if curious passers-by thought it rather strange to see this 'mature woman' having fun and games with a blue and orange kite, it did not deter her in the least.

Kite flying is considered a very scientific exercise, as well as great fun. With training and experience, new heights and wonders can be achieved, and I am told there are organizations, exhibitions, gatherings of one sort or another, all dedicated to kite flying, with mutual information and support for like-minded owners—although I doubt whether my basic kite and its owner would be considered fit to join such a body. But no matter, I like it, I have it, and who knows what I might progress to next?

A word that has crept or catapulted into our vocabulary in recent years is 'ageism', an awareness that people may be discriminated against because of their age rather than who they are and what they are capable of doing. It certainly happens in many aspects of our life, and so maybe drawing attention to it, even passing legislation about it, could be a good thing. But perhaps it is up to older people themselves to combat the fallacies that direct what older people can or cannot do or enjoy. What is 'older' in one person's opinion can be quite young in another. Age can prove very elastic; it depends on how much 'give' there is, how much enthusiasm, energy, dedication and vision a person has.

As I read scripture I see how God chose and used people well past their prime to accomplish great deeds, attain new heights, win battles, inspire new hope and thought. What about Noah, Abraham and Sarah, Moses, Zechariah and Elizabeth, Simeon and Anna? Think how much we owe to John, who in his old age, exiled on the island of Patmos, saw and shared the great vision of what was to come. These were all people who were open to the Holy Spirit of God, and who allowed him to take them in new directions, filled with his power, showing the way for others to follow.

So often we know within us the calling of God. We feel him pulling, disturbing, inviting us to action, but we hold back, we offer our feeble excuses, we claim age exclusion, and so we miss out on the adventure of service, the joy of experiencing new life. A popular expression today is 'If you don't use it you lose it'— relating to physical ability, mental agility, even your cash in hand. It applies equally to spiritual capacity, to the endless opportunities we have, at any age, of discovering new truths and sharing them, achieving new heights of awareness of God's grace and power, and being enabled to inspire others, to draw them into a deeper fellowship with him. It is happening all the time; I see it and hear it. I know from personal experience just what the so-called older people are doing and being. I asked one man recently just how he came to be able to achieve so much for God at his age. His eyes twinkled as he said, 'Availability!'

What has all this to do with flying a kite? When I fly my kite, as I see it take to the air, as I feel the pull in my hand, the exhilaration in my heart, it is a reminder of the wind of the Spirit blowing over all creation, the wind of the Spirit of recreation, the wind of the Spirit who invites us to 'come fly with me', to be part of his work of touching lives, changing them, drawing them to the one who makes all things new—at any age or at any stage of life.

We are not told how old Zacchaeus was when he had that life-changing experience of meeting Jesus personally, and being welcomed by him as a friend. I imagine he was 'getting on'. After all, he was a chief tax-collector, and rich, obviously an astute businessman, although in a very unsavoury business. Despised and hated by his fellow Jews for being employed by the occupying power, he needed to watch his step, to be careful where he went and what he did. Not the sort of man you would expect to go shinning up a tree—but then he was desperate to see Jesus for himself. He was changed completely, in a moment, by meeting with Jesus, and showed the evidence of the change by his practical response of generosity and restitution. It is often said that you cannot change the habits of a lifetime. Zacchaeus did! He 'flew a kite' by taking the invitation of Jesus with both hands. A free man with a whole new life, and a glorious future—and that can happen to anyone, anywhere, any time.

The 'wind of change' brings new life, breaking down the barriers of age, tradition, and inclination. We too can only marvel and enjoy the freedom it gives, the energy it provides as it draws us onward and upward, new-born into the kingdom of heaven. Our date of birth, the tally of years, our physical age, have nothing to do with our spiritual life. The onset of greying hair, stiffening limbs, fading eyesight and hearing, the need for spare parts, pills and potions, holds no power over the spirit, and if we come to the point of even forgetting who we are, God never does, and never will. He keeps his promise: 'Behold, I make all things new.'

Are there kites in heaven? I sometimes wonder, as I fly my earthly one, feel the wind in my face, the tug of the line. But maybe the answer is, 'Fly now, know later'; and I look forward with eager anticipation to the glorious fulfilment of God's promise, living life to the full as part of his new creation for ever.

Jesus entered Jericho and was passing through it. A man was there named Zacchaeus; he was a chief tax-collector and was rich. He was trying to see who Jesus was, but on account of the crowd he could not, because he was short in stature. So he ran ahead and climbed a sycamore tree to see him, because he was going to pass that way. When Jesus came to the place, he looked up and said to him, 'Zacchaeus, hurry and come down, for I must stay at your house today.' So he hurried down and was happy to welcome him. All who saw it began to grumble and said, 'He has gone to be the guest of one who is a sinner.' Zacchaeus stood there and said to the Lord, 'Look, half of my possessions, Lord, I will give to the poor; and if I have defrauded anyone of anything, I will pay back four times as much.' Then Jesus said to him, 'Today salvation has come to this house, because he too is a son of Abraham. For the Son of Man came to seek out and to save the lost.'

LUKE 19:1–10

Lord, the older I get, the more inclined I am to think I know it all. I have gone through the 'been there, done it, seen it, got the T-shirt' stage, and now I just smile sweetly when any new suggestions are made, or changes are mooted; for I know, or I think I know, that there is nothing new under heaven. It has all been tried before, life goes round in circles, as others will realize when they get to my age and know what I know. It is a comfortable state to be in, very safe and secure. My layers of self-protection have been built up over the years, my views and opinions formed, almost cast in stone… and yet… suddenly I feel a pulling and tugging at my heart, my soul, as I open up, just a fraction. The wind rushes in, disturbing me, upsetting my carefully arranged life, turning things round, pushing me, inviting me, almost dancing with me, making me see beyond the safe and secure vista to a new horizon, and I know that is the place to be.

How can I leave all that I have accumulated so carefully, all that I have laboured over, built up with such care? I cannot begin again, not now; but then what is there here that I really need? How can I get there, beyond the horizon? What form of transport can I hail for the journey? The wind enfolds me, wrapping me into its embrace, and carries me up. Like a kite I fly, bursting with an energy not of my making or understanding. And now I know what it is to be truly myself, and truly part of you, released by the wind of your Spirit, yet held safe and secure by your hand of love and power. I am born again, reborn to share the new heaven and earth, part of your kingdom of renewed creation, of all things and all people made new. I am a child of your love through Jesus, brought home by your Spirit. Father, Son and Holy Spirit, I am made one with you—for ever.

And the one who was seated on the throne said, 'See, I am making all things new.'
REVELATION 21:5

Other Christina Press titles

Who'd Plant a Church? Diana Archer
£5.99 in UK
Planting an Anglican church from scratch, with a team of four—
two adults and two children—is an unusual adventure even in
these days. Diana Archer is a vicar's wife who gives a distinctive
perspective on parish life.

Pathway Through Grief edited by Jean Watson
£6.99 in UK
Ten Christians, each bereaved, share their experience of loss.
Frank and sensitive accounts offering comfort and reassurance
to those recently bereaved. Jean Watson has lost her own husband and believes that those involved in counselling will also
gain new insights from these honest personal chronicles.

God's Catalyst Rosemary Green
£8.99 in UK
Rosemary Green's international counselling ministry has prayer
and listening to God at its heart. Changed lives and rekindled
faith testify to God's healing power. Here she provides insight,
inspiration and advice for both counsellors and concerned
Christians who long to be channels of God's Spirit to help those
in need. *God's Catalyst* is a unique tool for the non-specialist
counsellor; for the pastor who has no training; for the Christian
who wants to come alongside hurting friends.

Angels Keep Watch Carol Hathorne
£5.99 in UK
A true adventure showing how God still directs our lives, not
with wind, earthquake or fire, but by the still, small voice.
    'Go to Africa.' The Lord had been saying it for over fory years.
At last, Carol Hathorne had obeyed, going out to Kenya with her
husband. On the eastern side of Nairobi, where tourists never
go, they came face to face with dangers, hardships and poverty
on a daily basis, but experienced the joy of learning that
Christianity is still growing in God's world.

Not a Super-Saint Liz Hansford
£6.99 in UK
'You might have thought Adrian Plass... had cornered the market in amusing diary writing. Well, check out Liz Hansford's often hilarious account of life as a Baptist minister's wife in Belfast. Highly recommended.' *The New Christian Herald*

Liz Hansford describes the outlandish situations which arise in the Manse, where life is both fraught and tremendous fun. *Not a Super-Saint* is for the ordinary Christian who feels they must be the only one who hasn't quite got it all together.

The Addiction of a Busy Life Edward England
£5.99 in UK
Twelve lessons from a devastating heart attack. Edward, a giant of Christian publishing in the UK, and founder of Christina Press, shares what the Lord taught him when his life nearly came to an abrupt end. Although not strictly a Christina title (Edward lacks the gender qualifications), we believe you may want to buy this for the busy men in your lives.

'A wonderful story of success and frailty, of love and suffering, of despair and hope. If you are too busy to read this book, you are too busy.' *Dr Michael Green*

Life Path Luci Shaw
£5.99 in UK
Personal and spiritual growth through journal writing. Life has a way of slipping out of the back door while we're not looking. Keeping a journal can enrich life as we live it, and bring it all back later. Luci Shaw shows how a journal can also help us grow in our walk with God.

Precious to God Sarah Bowen
£5.99 in UK
Two young people, delighted to be starting a family, have their expectations shattered by the arrival of a handicapped child. And yet this is only the first of many difficulties to be faced. What was initially a tragedy is, through faith, transformed into a story of inspiration, hope and spiritual enrichment.

All the above titles are available from Christian bookshops everywhere, or in case of difficulty, direct from Christina Press using the order form on page 156.

Other BRF titles

Still Time for Eternity Margaret Cundiff
£5.99 in UK
In the midst of our busyness, and the even greater rush of the wider world, there are few times when we stand still long enough to see the big picture, the working of God's kingdom values here on earth.

Taking a series of 'snapshots' over time from the winding up of the last century and the beginning of this one, Margaret Cundiff reflects on how we can discover God's love and concern in action. She brings together reflections on Scripture with events in everyday life, as well as in the newspapers and TV bulletins. What we find is that these moments, captured in the heart for whatever reason, are worth a second look before we all dash on. After all, there is still time for eternity—and that's what really matters.

The Road through the Desert Alison Jacobs
Making sense of wilderness times
£5.99 in UK
Feeling emotionally and spiritually dry? In some way defeated? Even despairing?

Many people—both Christians and non-believers—feel alienated not only from God but from the world in which they live, either through some kind of loss or difficulty, or simply because each day seems like one big struggle. This is no new problem! *The Road through the Desert* is a practical and thought-provoking guide which follows Moses and the Israelites on their Old Testament wilderness wanderings, drawing out lessons to help to bring today's 'wilderness travellers' into the Promised Land that God has ready for them.

'An interesting and challenging read... I am sure it will prove helpful to those struggling with their own personal wilderness times.' (Bridget Plass)

With Jesus in the Upper Room David Winter
Forty gospel reflections for Lent and Easter
£6.99 in UK

This book, BRF's Lent book for 2002, invites us to spend forty days reflecting on five key chapters of John's Gospel, the so-called 'Upper Room Discourses' which record the conversation between Jesus and his disciples on the night before he died. As we read, we can imagine ourselves sitting with those disciples as the darkness falls outside while the light among them grows brighter and brighter. Through the ears, eyes and memory of the 'Beloved Disciple' who recalled what took place long after the event, we can share in the wonder of a quite extraordinary evening.

The Easter Experience Rachel Heathfield
Growing with God through Jesus' Easter story
£3.99 in UK

Jesus' Easter story means that we never ever need to be separated from God. Being apart from God is a bit like us having a bit missing, like a teddy without an eye or a bike without a wheel. But because of Jesus we can be God's friends for ever—which is exactly what God has always wanted!

Children aged 5–7 can read this book on their own or with a friend or family member. Inside they'll find things to think about and do, with Bible verses to show them the way and their very own prayer jotter to help them get to know Jesus better as they learn about his Easter experience.

This book is the latest in the 'Beginning with God' series. Also available are *Belonging to God*, *Believing in God*, *See for Yourself* and *Stars at Night*.

All the above titles are available from Christian bookshops everywhere or, in case of difficulty, direct from BRF using the order form on page 157.

Christina Press Publications Order Form

All of these publications are available from Christian bookshops everywhere or, in case of difficulty, direct from the publisher. Please make your selection below, complete the payment details and send your order with payment as appropriate to:

Christina Press Ltd, 17 Church Road, Tunbridge Wells, Kent TN1 1LG

		Qty	Price	Total
8700	God's Catalyst	____	£8.99	____
8702	Precious to God	____	£5.99	____
8703	Angels Keep Watch	____	£5.99	____
8704	Life Path	____	£5.99	____
8705	Pathway Through Grief	____	£6.99	____
8706	Who'd Plant a Church?	____	£5.99	____
8708	Not a Super-Saint	____	£6.99	____
8705	The Addiction of a Busy Life	____	£5.99	____

POSTAGE AND PACKING CHARGES				
	UK	Europe	Surface	Air Mail
£7.00 & under	£1.25	£2.25	£2.25	£3.50
£7.10–£29.99	£2.25	£5.50	£7.50	£11.00
£30.00 & over	free	prices on request		

Total cost of books £ _____
Postage and Packing £ _____
TOTAL £ _____

All prices are correct at time of going to press, are subject to the prevailing rate of VAT and may be subject to change without prior warning.

Name _____

Address _____

_____

_____ Postcode _____

Total enclosed £ _____ (cheques should be made payable to 'Christina Press Ltd')

☐ Please send me further information about Christina Press publications

BRF Publications Order Form

All of these publications are available from Christian bookshops everywhere, or in case of difficulty direct from the publisher. Please make your selection below, complete the payment details and send your order with payment as appropriate to:

BRF, First Floor, Elsfield Hall, 15–17 Elsfield Way, Oxford OX2 8FG

		Qty	Price	Total
212 2	Still Time for Eternity		£5.99	
138 X	The Road through the Desert		£5.99	
213 0	With Jesus in the Upper Room		£6.99	
219 X	The Easter Experience		£3.99	
101 0	Stars at Night		£3.99	
102 9	See for Yourself		£3.99	
103 7	Belonging to God		£3.99	
104 5	Believing in God		£3.99	

POSTAGE AND PACKING CHARGES				
	UK	Europe	Surface	Air Mail
£7.00 & under	£1.25	£2.25	£2.25	£3.50
£7.10–£29.99	£2.25	£5.50	£7.50	£11.00
£30.00 & over	free	prices on request		

Total cost of books   £ _____

Postage and Packing   £ _____

TOTAL   £ _____

All prices are correct at time of going to press, are subject to the prevailing rate of VAT and may be subject to change without prior warning.

Name _____

Address _____

_____

_____ Postcode _____

Total enclosed £ _____ (cheques should be made payable to 'BRF')

Payment by: cheque ❑ postal order ❑ Visa ❑ Mastercard ❑ Switch ❑

Card no. ❑❑❑❑❑❑❑❑❑❑❑❑❑❑❑❑

Card expiry date ❑❑❑❑   Issue number (Switch) ❑❑❑❑

Signature _____

(essential if paying by credit/Switch card)

❑ Please send me further information about BRF publications

Visit the BRF website at www.brf.org.uk

Subscription Information

Each issue of *Day by Day with God* is available from Christian book-shops everywhere. Copies may also be available through your church Book Agent or from the person who distributes Bible reading notes in your church.

Alternatively you may obtain *Day by Day with God* on subscription direct from the publishers. There are two kinds of subscription:

Individual Subscriptions are for four copies or less, and include postage and packing. To order an annual Individual Subscription please complete the details on page 160 and send the coupon with payment to BRF in Oxford. You can also use the form to order a Gift Subscription for a friend. ·

Church Subscriptions are for five copies or more, sent to one address, and are supplied post free. Church Subscriptions run from 1 May to 30 April each year and are invoiced annually. To order a Church Subscription please complete the details opposite and send the coupon to BRF in Oxford. You will receive an invoice with the first issue of notes.

All subscription enquiries should be directed to:

BRF
First Floor
Elsfield Hall
15–17 Elsfield Way
Oxford
OX2 8FG

Tel: 01865 319700
Fax: 01865 319701
E-mail: subscriptions@brf.org.uk

Church Subscriptions

The Church Subscription rate for *Day by Day with God* will be £9.90 per person until April 2003.

☐ I would like to take out a church subscription for _____ (Qty) copies.

☐ Please start my order with the May/September 2002/January 2003* issue.
I would like to pay annually/receive an invoice with each edition of the notes*.
(*Please delete as appropriate)

Please do not send any money with your order. Send your order to BRF and we will send you an invoice. The Church Subscription year is from May to April. If you start subscribing in the middle of a subscription year we will invoice you for the remaining number of issues left in that year.

Name and address of the person organising the Church Subscription:

Name _____

Address _____

_____

_____

Postcode _____ Telephone _____

Church _____

Name of Minister _____

Name and address of the person paying the invoice if the invoice needs to be sent directly to them:

Name _____

Address _____

_____

_____

Postcode _____ Telephone _____

Please send your coupon to:

BRF
First Floor
Elsfield Hall
15–17 Elsfield Way
Oxford
OX2 8FG

DBDWG0102   BRF is a Registered Charity

Individual Subscriptions

☐ I would like to give a gift subscription (please complete both name and address sections below)

☐ I would like to take out a subscription myself (complete name and address details only once)

The completed coupon should be sent with appropriate payment to BRF. Alternatively, please write to us quoting your name, address, the subscription you would like for either yourself or a friend (with their name and address), the start date and credit card number, expiry date and signature if paying by credit card.

Gift subscription name _____

Gift subscription address _____

_____ Postcode_____

Please send to the above for one year, beginning with the May/September 2002/ January 2003 issue: (delete as applicable)

	UK	Surface	Air Mail
Day by Day with God	☐ £11.55	☐ £12.90	☐ £15.15
2-year subscription	☐ £19.99	N/A	N/A

Please complete the payment details below and send your coupon, with appropriate payment, to BRF, First Floor, Elsfield Hall, 15–17 Elsfield Way, Oxford OX2 8FG

Your name _____

Your address _____

_____ Postcode_____

Total enclosed £ _____ (cheques should be made payable to 'BRF')
Payment by: cheque ☐ postal order ☐ Visa ☐ Mastercard ☐ Switch ☐

Card no. ☐☐☐☐☐☐☐☐☐☐☐☐☐☐☐☐☐☐

Card expiry date ☐☐☐☐   Issue number (Switch) ☐☐☐☐

Signature _____

(essential if paying by credit/Switch card)

NB: These notes are also available from Christian bookshops everywhere.

DBDWG0102   BRF is a Registered Charity